MIRACLES

Healing for a Broken World

Fr. Stefan Starzynski
with Chris Grzasko

MIRACLES
Healing for a Broken World

Our Sunday Visitor Publishing Division
Our Sunday Visitor, Inc.
Huntington, Indiana 46750

Nihil Obstat: Msgr. Michael Heintz, Ph.D.
Censor Librorum
Imprimatur: ✠Kevin C. Rhoades
Bishop of Fort Wayne-South Bend
February 22, 2010

The *Nihil Obstat* and *Imprimatur* are official declarations that a book or pamphlet is free of doctrinal or moral error. No implication is contained therein that those who have granted the *Nihil Obstat* or *Imprimatur* agree with the contents, opinions, or statements expressed.

Except where otherwise indicated, the Scripture citations used in this work are taken from the *Catholic Edition of the Revised Standard Version of the Bible (RSV)*, copyright © 1965 and 1966 by the Division of Christian Education of the National Council of the Churches of Christ in the United States of America. Used by permission. All rights reserved.

Some Scripture excerpts are taken from the *New American Bible with Revised New Testament and Psalms,* copyright © 1991, 1986, 1970, Confraternity of Christian Doctrine, Inc., Washington, D.C. Used with permission. All rights reserved. No part of the *New American Bible* may be reproduced by any means without permission in writing from the copyright owner.

Every reasonable effort has been made to determine copyright holders of excerpted materials and to secure permissions as needed. If any copyrighted materials have been inadvertently used in this work without proper credit being given in one form or another, please notify Our Sunday Visitor in writing so that future printings of this work may be corrected accordingly.

Our Sunday Visitor Publishing Division
Our Sunday Visitor, Inc.
200 Noll Plaza
Huntington, IN 46750
1-800-348-2440
bookpermissions@osv.com

ISBN: 978-1-59276-716-8 (Inventory No. T1037)
LCCN: 2010921393

Cover design by Lindsey Luken
Cover photo: Shutterstock
Interior design by Sherri L. Hoffman

PRINTED IN THE UNITED STATES OF AMERICA

CONTENTS

In Memory of Paul Stefan, Jacob, Mary, Monica,
St. Thérèse the Little Flower,
and Our Lady of Guadalupe

Unless you are willing to do the ridiculous, God will not do the miraculous.

— MOTHER ANGELICA

FOREWORD

The longing to satisfy the desires of our hearts and fill the void when life seems empty stirs in us ceaselessly. For life to be purposeful, it must travel on the spiritual network of hope, faith, and love that, in turn, activates the daily miracles we experience. With all the divergent "-isms" of today, such as consumerism, nepotism, and tribalism, our fragile world is broken, and the sublime presence of God's love has been overtaken by the vague promises of the world. Turning to the world engenders doubt, active despair, and hatred for a world created out of God's love.

In the face of war, violence, abortion, and the stark reality of incurable diseases, many people have run out of reasons to believe in the existence of God and miracles, and are thus on the verge of believing the future is hopeless. This necessitates the thought-provoking question: Where is God in the face of all this, and are miracles still possible in our broken world?

The existential miracles that have happened through Fr. Stefan have become a new flame of hope set to rekindle the mind of the contemporary Christian and a world in desperate need of hope. In the power of the Holy Spirit and assisted by prayer, the Church has always sought to heal the human condition, particularly through her liturgy and teachings. Today, the Holy Spirit is actively working through his ministers, bringing healing that stands the test of time by word, thought, and presence.

Fr. Stefan's prolific work remains a landmark accomplishment that transcends theoretical or mere abstract ideologies. It is an existential experience that has proven itself. As he relates his experiences, he captures the nucleus of the very expression of faith that each believer hopes to attain. Testimonies emerge from personal experience and go beyond mere coincidence. Having been critically examined with the lens of objective truth in line with the teachings of the Church, the testimonies in this book are above reproach and have consequently become a source of inspiration for the faithful.

The chapters relate the overwhelming impact of miracles as a vehicle of healing to a broken world. Fr. Stefan has been able to show the active presence of the Holy Spirit in every area of our lives. All God expects from us is to be open to the promptings and direction of the Holy Spirit with all amount of humility.

Fr. Stefan's approach to this book is lucid and simple. It is designed to edify the educated laity, rekindle the faith of the clergy and those who live with despair; to inspire the tepid preacher to flames of desire, and energize the kerygmatic followers of Christ to become aware of the inner dynamisms of the faith that can help them connect with God. This is an engaging book that, once picked up, is not easily laid down again. I recommend it highly, as it will quench the thirst of a restless heart and fill our emptiness with the Spirit, revealing the invitation of Christ, who is the ultimate fulfillment of one's spiritual thirst.

— FR. BONIFACE EWAH

ACKNOWLEDGMENTS

I would like to thank Chris Grzasko for all her hard work; this book would not have seen the light of day without her. I can be very scattered in my thoughts, and it took a very patient and kind person to assemble and organize my stories. I think back to the day that Chris came up to St. Mary's to offer help to write this book and am grateful that she has been true to her word. One day during the summer of 2008, I asked Chris how much time she spent working on this book. She told me she worked on it eight hours a day. May the good Jesus bless her for all her hard work. God bless!

Chris would like to thank Diana Branscome, Colleen Turgeon, Mary Jo Medosch, Carly Medosch, Mary O'Neill, and all those who gave support during the writing of this book.

NOTE

The experiences and events recounted in this book are my own and those of the persons whom I have encountered, worked with, and prayed with. (In some instances, names have been changed for privacy's sake.) Nothing I have written in the following pages should be construed to be the positions or policies of the Diocese of Arlington. As St. Francis de Sales said:

> I submit all my writings, my words, and actions to the correction of the most holy Catholic, Apostolic, and Roman Church, knowing that she is the pillar and ground of truth, wherein she can neither be deceived nor deceive us, and that none can have God for his father who will not have this Church for his Mother.
>
> — FR. STEFAN STARZYNSKI

INTRODUCTION

Fr. Stefan Starzynski

The inspiration for this book came one day when Chris Grzasko and Jill Bender came to take me out to dinner before a healing Mass. At dinner, they told me that they thought I ought to write a book to relate all the wonderful things that Jesus has done in my life and in the lives of others.

Our God is a life-giving God, a God that wants us to have life and have it more abundantly, a God that wants to show us that He loves us. As Jesus says:

> "What man of you, if his son asks him for bread, will give him a stone? Or if he asks for a fish, will give him a serpent? If you then, who are evil, know how to give good gifts to your children, how much more will your Father who is in heaven give good things to those who ask him!"
>
> — Mt 7:9-11

Our good Father in heaven is just waiting to show us how much he loves us.

Our God is not a sad God, but a God full of life, love, and fun. What is more fun than celebrating by having a margarita with friends after you have experienced the love of Jesus and been touched by His miracles?

Why are miracles important? We live in an unbelieving time. It is readily accepted that God worked miracles in the early Church to convert pagan Rome and to establish his Church. I personally believe that Jesus never intended his miracles to lessen or cease, but we slowly began to accept the idea that miracles are rare in the Church; they are usually associated with very holy men and women or holy places such as Lourdes, France. Many people concluded, "I'm not a saint, so Jesus won't work a miracle through me." So, with this belief came a reduction in the number of miracles.

I believe that Jesus is once again moving his hand to work great signs and wonders among his people to awaken a skeptical age. Our present day is at least as pagan as ancient Rome. Even if we accept the idea that Jesus worked his miracles to convert a pagan Rome and establish the Church, doesn't it make sense that Jesus would work his miracles today to awaken a pagan age and show us that yes, he is alive? That he is the same yesterday, today, and forever?

In this book, I have given my own testimony and included testimonies of others. Why are testimonies important? We have only to reflect on Jesus' healing of the ten lepers. Only one came back to give thanks. Giving thanks for the miracles that Jesus works in our life is a part of the healing. By giving testimony, we confirm before others that Jesus has worked in our lives. May we always be like the grateful leper who came back and gave thanks so that we might hear from Jesus, "Rise and go your way; your faith has made you well" (Lk 17:19).

It is important to give some reflection on the healing Mass itself. Actually, it's more properly referred to as a Mass and healing service. First, we have the Mass, and then we have the prayer service. The prayer service consists of testimonies of people who have been touched by the Holy Spirit or have received a miracle. Testimonies are important because we all need to hear how God has worked through our lives. One priest says it this way: "If you don't have a testimony, you don't have a message."

After testimonies, we pray over people — and, despite what many people may think, there really is no magical formula for doing this. The most important ingredient is the faith of the person involved. I remember a reflection given by Fr. Raniero Cantalamessa, personal preacher to Pope John Paul II, in which he says that it is by our faith, not our virtue, that we receive God's blessings. It also does not depend on how good we are. Faith is the door by which we receive God's gifts. This is the reason that when I pray, I pray for big things.

In *The Diary of St. Faustina,* Jesus said to Sister Faustina of the Sisters of Our Lady of Mercy:

> The more a soul trusts, the more it will receive. Souls that trust boundlessly are a great comfort to Me, because I pour all the treasures of My graces into them. I rejoice that they ask for much, because it is My desire to give much, very much. On the other hand, I am sad when souls ask for little, when they narrow their hearts.
>
> — *DIARY,* 1578

Matthew 18:3 tells us, "Unless you turn and become like children, you will never enter the kingdom of heaven." Don't children ask for the stars? Don't children say to their parents, "When I grow up, I am going to give you a castle to live in"? Children think and dream big. Jesus wants us to do the same with him. "Ask, and it will be given you; seek, and you will find; knock, and it will be opened to you" (Mt 7:7).

I first connected the Mass with healing when I read a book by Fr. John Bertolucci titled *The Mass and Healing.* He brought to my attention for the first time how many references there are to healing in the Mass. But then you may ask, if every Mass is a healing Mass, why do I celebrate a special healing Mass? In response to this question, I often ask another one: "Why do people go to Lourdes to obtain healing?"

One reason is that Mary, the Mother of God, is present in a special way at Lourdes. But another reason, and I think a more important one, is that people's faith is stimulated at Lourdes. They come to Lourdes with faith; once there, they see all the sick people who have been touched by God and receive his healing, and their own faith is increased. (Still yet another reason is that by virtue of the fact that someone takes a week off from work, parts with

$1,000 for the trip, and endures the hardships of going to Lourdes, they expect to receive something from God!)

The healing Mass, then, is like going to Lourdes. Although every Mass is a healing Mass, people go to a Mass and healing service hoping to be touched by Jesus. They are also surrounded by hundreds of other people who believe in the healing power of Jesus. They hear the testimonies of people who have been healed. The expectant faith and the testimonies help create an atmosphere conducive to healing.

My first exposure to healing Masses was concelebrating them with Fr. McAlear and Fr. Tuck Grinnell. Fr. McAlear was my spiritual advisor and the one who baptized me in the Holy Spirit; he used to celebrate a monthly healing Mass. I also learned at the feet of Fr. Tuck Grinnell, who faithfully celebrates a monthly healing Mass in the Diocese of Arlington. Early in my priesthood, I would often concelebrate with him. During this period, I was learning and not yet ready to go off on my own.

When I was at St. Mary in Fredericksburg, Virginia, I asked Fr. Hamilton, my pastor, if I could celebrate a healing Mass in the parish. His first response was to ask me if I would have strength to do a healing Mass *and* Masses in the parish. Reflecting on his comment in prayer, I was led to the book of Daniel.

I read how Daniel was captured by King Nebuchadnezzar of Babylon and put in prison. In the story, the king's attendant brought meat for Daniel to eat. Daniel, being a good Jew, would touch nothing of the meat. He told the attendant to bring him vegetables instead. The king's attendant was reluctant because if Daniel looked weak by comparison to the other prisoners, the attendant would be punished, perhaps killed. Daniel made a deal with him: he asked the attendant to bring him vegetables for a week, and if after a week, he looked weak by comparison, he would eat the meat. After the week, however, Daniel looked stronger than those who ate only meat (see Dan 1:8-20).

I understood this passage — given to me by the Lord — to mean that while the healing Masses would take much time, I would find myself having *more* energy after the healing Masses, not less.

Six years later, I still find that to be true. While I have often found myself very tired after some healing Masses, I have also found that praying for people gives me strength and energy. It's wonderful when you see someone touched by God or healed. I have found that seeing and experiencing God's miracles, in myself and others, has increased my faith and given me more energy.

Since I have started celebrating the healing Masses, I continue to feel personally called by Jesus to do so. When I look back over my life, I find it beautiful that the first sacrament I administered on my ordination day, the Anointing of the Sick, resulted in a miracle (A.J.'s healing). I look back to that day and see that God was preparing me to pray for the healing of others. I realize as well that A.J.'s healing on my ordination day was also God preparing me to start the Paul Stefan Home for Expectant Mothers one day.

When you read this book, you will read the stories of many healings of babies. When I pray for babies, they are healed at a high rate; some people think it's because babies are so innocent. I believe it has also been God's way of preparing me to start homes for expectant mothers and their babies. How beautiful are the ways of the Lord!

I have also witnessed that when I pray for people with cancer, they also seem to be healed at a greater rate. There is much I don't understand, and I am still learning. A priest friend of mine never understood why when he prayed for people, their teeth would be healed. Later it struck him that before he became a priest, he had planned on being a dentist.

I pray that this book will help you believe that "with God all things are possible" (Mt 19:26) — that He can do wonders through us when we have faith. But always keep in mind that God is the healer; I am only His imperfect instrument. I do believe that I have a charism of healing, but it is God who gave it, and all glory goes to God. In my experience, the more healing that takes place, the more obvious it becomes that it is God who is working through me.

1

MY VOCATION

While I was attending Gannon University, I had been doing a Holy Hour every day, or at least spending time praying in front of the Blessed Sacrament. While I was in the chapel praying one Monday, I promised Jesus that I would pray a Rosary every single day of my life. That was in December of 1990 or January of 1991. I've kept that promise. In seventeen years, I've never missed a day of praying the Rosary. Making that promise was the moment I first knew that God was truly calling me to be a Catholic priest.

The summer after leaving college, I worked with Mother Teresa for two months in two different places. One was a house for the suffering and the other a home for the dying, with all the volunteers — including me — working alongside the Missionaries of Charity. Mother Teresa gave each volunteer a specific person to care for. I cared for a man who was covered in bedsores. Every morning, I cleaned his sores and every day, I washed him. It was a very humbling experience.

I hadn't expected my encounter with working with Mother Teresa and her Sisters to be such a religious experience. I didn't realize how much of the service that the Missionaries of Charity provide is rooted in prayer. I joined the nuns every morning for prayer and Mass, and we closed every day with Holy Hour. Once a week, we had a private audience with Mother Teresa.

One of the things I remember Mother Teresa saying was that they had never gone without food. As we went to the Home for the Dying, our job was to pick up dinner for the residents of the home; but on one particular day, there was a riot of the Muslim population and because of that, there was no dinner. I was the only one who knew that, and I thought, "Let us put Mother's words to the test."

At the Home for the Dying, about a half an hour before dinnertime, the doorbell rang. It was a man from a local restaurant who wanted to know if we could use the extra food from his restaurant. Mother was right. God provides!

Every day, I would see Mother Teresa kneeling in front of the Blessed Sacrament. One day when I was walking around the convent, I bumped into her. It was just the two of us, and I asked her to pray three Hail Marys for my vocation. She did. It was during this time that I was anticipating receiving word of my acceptance into the seminary. I clearly remember that day in India when I got the call to say that I had been accepted!

Two weeks before my ordination, I was in my room praying. I said, "Jesus, do you want me to be a priest? Jesus, should I stay here?" Then I pulled the Bible off the shelf and opened it at random. This was the first time I had ever done this. The Scripture verses I opened to were Acts 1:4-8, in which Jesus tells his apostles to stay in Jerusalem, and . . .

"You shall receive power when the Holy Spirit has come upon you; and you shall be my witnesses in Jerusalem and in all Judea and Samaria and to the end of the earth."

Jesus spoke these words to the apostles as he ascended into heaven, nine days before Pentecost. I was convinced that Jesus had spoken to me through his word. I had asked if I should stay, and Jesus responded, "Yes."

––––––––––

Before going on retreat to prepare for ordination, I read a book written by Ralph Martin that changed my life — *The Catholic*

Church at the End of an Age: What Is the Spirit Saying? Martin bases his book on John 12:32, where Jesus said, "And I, when I am lifted up from the earth, will draw all men to myself." The verse hit me like a lightning bolt. I realized that my vocation as a priest was to proclaim Jesus, to lift up the Person of Jesus, so that people would be drawn to him, not to me.

In the second half of the book, Martin writes about the Baptism of the Holy Spirit. I had never heard of it before. He said Baptism in the Holy Spirit is a release of the graces that were given to us at baptism. The more I read about this, the more I wanted to receive that baptism.

So on May 18, 1996, at my ordination, when I was lying down in front of the bishop, I said a prayer to Jesus in my heart: "Jesus, I know I'm going to be a priest in the sacramental sense, but I want to be baptized in the Holy Spirit, too. I need this Holy Spirit."

After the ordination, while I was at my parents' house for a reception, two very special things happened.

At my parents' house is a pergola for grapevines to grow over the patio. During the party I went outside and, as if on cue, from out of nowhere, a white dove came out of the sky and landed right over my head. My uncle, who doesn't believe in anything religious, was struck. He was the one who first brought it to my attention. The white dove is a symbol of the Holy Spirit. I had never seen a white dove outdoors before, and it stayed there for as long as I was outside. When I went back inside, it left.

The second special event on my ordination day began when my friend Mary Beth came to me and said that her next door neighbor's baby was deathly ill. She asked if I would go and anoint the baby.

I left the party and went to the hospital. I saw this little baby with tubes and wires all over the place and learned that he had never left the hospital in six months. I said to the mom and dad, "Do you believe that if I anoint your baby, that your baby will be healed?" (No one had yet told me that these things don't happen!) They answered, "Yes. We believe."

I anointed Allen — they called him A.J. for short. Three days later, someone from the family called to tell me that Allen was miraculously healed. I wasn't even surprised. "Isn't this what we expected?" I said.

Later, because of the healing of their son, the couple — who both were in a second marriage at the time — would seek annulments of their first marriages. I performed their wedding. After the wedding ceremony, the couple told me how the hospital personnel became frantic six years earlier when all the machinery was going haywire. The reason it was going haywire? Allen was breathing by himself.

Two days after my ordination, I went to a healing service. In the chapel, Fr. McAlear and about twelve other people placed their hands on me. Then Fr. McAlear did something I had never heard of before; he started praying in tongues. The first reading at Mass that night was from the Acts of the Apostles:

> And when Paul laid his hands upon them, the Holy Spirit came on them, and they spoke in tongues and prophesied.
>
> — ACTS 19:6

I felt the Holy Spirit go through me from my head to my toes, and I knew at that moment that I was forever changed. I remember feeling joyful, like all of heaven was opened up and poured into me. It wasn't until later that I learned that what I had experienced had a name — the Baptism of the Holy Spirit I had prayed for.

Not long after, during my first parish assignment, I myself received the gift of tongues through the help of a Protestant minister — which shows that Baptism in the Holy Spirit is an ecumenical phenomenon, and the Holy Spirit blows where he may.

2

BABY MIRACLES

The Lord has shown me the power of the sacraments, especially the power of baptism. When I first became a priest, I never understood why, whenever I prayed over babies, they were healed. Many times I've been called to the hospital to baptize a baby who is about to die. On many occasions, I've witnessed the little ones suddenly and miraculously get better. Baptism imparts divine life into the soul, and that divine life conquers the illness.

Once while I was at St. Mary's in Alexandria, I was walking along the Potomac River bike path in Old Towne when a man near me got off his bike and said, "Fr. Stefan, I want you to know that you are the reason I became Catholic."

"Oh, that's nice." I replied.

"Last year —" he began.

I interrupted, "I always like when people say 'last year.' It means they have been listening for awhile, and something stuck!"

He went on to tell me that he was an Episcopalian at the time, and his wife was Catholic. They had brought their baby boy to me to be baptized the year before — an event I didn't recall, but he was glad to recount to me.

At that time, the boy had bandages all over his throat. After the baptism, I had asked the parents if it was okay for me to remove the bandages from the baby's neck and pour the holy water over his throat. They agreed to let me do this.

The baby was scheduled to have surgery on his throat to correct either a breathing or an eating difficulty, and the idea of surgery on their newborn baby was a horrific thought for them. However, when they took their son to the doctor to schedule the surgery, a few days after the baptism, the doctor told them that their baby was perfectly healed. As a result of seeing his child healed through the sacrament of Baptism, the father decided to become Catholic.

Another time, I was called to Fairfax Hospital to visit a pregnant woman who was on bed rest. The baby's grandparents had asked me to come to the hospital to anoint their daughter, Sharon, who was about sixteen weeks pregnant. Sharon would have to be in the hospital for the remainder of her pregnancy. I went to the hospital and anointed Sharon. A few days later, I went back to the hospital to visit her again, and was surprised that she had been released.

The next day at church, Sharon's parents told me that after I anointed her, the doctor came in and looked at a sonogram. He said, "How beautiful, your baby is kneeling in your womb as if in prayer." The doctor didn't even know I had been there to anoint Sharon. Almost like John the Baptist, who leapt in the womb in the presence of Jesus, the baby had responded to grace. The anointing healed the mother and saved the baby's life. Six months later, I baptized this baby.

In Alexandria Hospital, another woman was also in the hospital on bed rest at about sixteen weeks into her pregnancy. Labor had begun, but the doctors were hoping to keep the baby in the womb for as long as they possibly could. I prayed with the mother that the baby would wait as long as possible before being born.

I don't remember the exact number of weeks that passed before the baby was delivered, but I do know the baby was in the safe realm — premature but viable enough to be out of the womb.

Even as the baby was being delivered, the doctors tried to prevent the delivery, but the baby forced himself out.

Then, within minutes after the baby was delivered, the mother began hemorrhaging. If the baby had remained in the womb even a few minutes longer, he would have died due to the hemorrhaging. God had answered the prayer so beautifully, keeping the baby in the womb for the longest possible time needed for development. Yet, five more minutes in the womb, and the baby would have died.

I had a dream in which a poor woman gave me a baby and said, "Fr. Stefan, take my baby. I trust you to find a family for my baby. And by the way, his name is Samuel."

Some friends of mine, Julie and Ruffin, were looking to adopt a baby. I told Julie about my dream, and I told her that I would give her this baby whose name was Samuel.

Julie called me back a few weeks later in tears. "Fr. Stefan, guess what?" she said. "I am holding my new baby, Samuel." God had provided her with a baby, and because of my dream, they named him Jack Samuel. A few weeks later, I went to St. Mary's and baptized their beautiful baby boy.

Jack Samuel is now over a year old and doing very well, and his parents have given him a wonderful home.

Susan, a preschool teacher and her husband, Tom, a gym coach, were a couple I knew fairly well. But one day, I got a call from Tom saying, "Quick! You've got to get to the hospital. Susan is giving birth" — and I was completely taken aback. I thought, *Giving birth?* Susan was a very petite person, and nobody even knew she was pregnant. They hadn't told anyone, and I had no idea she was expecting.

I felt honored that Susan had asked me to be at the hospital, so I hurried there. When I got there, I learned that the night before,

Susan's placenta had separated from the wall of the womb, and she had lost a lot of blood, as much as five or six pints. The doctors were only giving her a 50-50 chance of living. It didn't look good for the baby, either.

Tom was pacing, frantic about his wife and his baby and unable to comprehend possibly losing them both on the same day. Tom and I prayed the Rosary together outside the room.

I entered Susan's room then and gave her the Anointing of the Sick. I felt in my heart and soul that she would be fine. Then, I went to see the baby — without knowing that in fact, the baby boy had been born dead at 25½ weeks, weighing only one pound, fourteen ounces. The doctors had had to resuscitate him before Tom and I went into the room.

As we looked at the baby, because of all the people I'd seen healed through baptism, I said that this infant would be healed through the holiness of God; the baptism would conquer his infirmities. I asked Tom what name I should give the baby when I baptized him. He responded, "James."

I replied, "Oh, good! James is a strong name." Then I baptized him and said to Tom, "He's going to be all right."

Shortly thereafter, I celebrated a healing Mass and offered it for Susan and baby James. During the intentions, everyone present heard a voice — an angel's voice — say, "Pray for Susan and her baby."

Baby James remained in the hospital in Richmond for a couple of months. The students at school prayed for him daily, and to this day, James is known as the "Miracle Baby" among the students. I believe it was through his baptism and through the students' faithful prayers that James received God's healing.

James is a very healthy and active little boy. No one would ever know that he fought a battle at birth.

———

I gave a talk one day about healing to a group of home-schooling families and shared the story about baby Allen's healing on my ordination day. Then, I mentioned to them one of the events that changed the way I thought about healing.

Fr. Raniero Cantalamessa, the preacher to Pope John Paul II, posed the question, "Where do miracles come from? Do they come from Jesus' divinity?" Fr. Cantalamessa said no, that miracles come from the Holy Spirit, working through Jesus' humanity. And we receive that same Holy Spirit. It is very beautiful to know that we are called to bestow God's miracles in the same way that Jesus did. Jesus promises us this in the Gospel of John:

> "Truly, truly, I say to you, he who believes in me will also do the works that I do; and greater works than these will he do, because I go to the Father."
>
> — JN 14:12

A mother named Theresa heard my talk that day. She had recently given birth to a little girl named Emily who was born with Down syndrome. After hearing my talk, Theresa and her husband, Mark, were inspired to ask me to pray over Emily.

Later, Emily was diagnosed with leukemia. I would learn that Down syndrome and leukemia are often connected. For Theresa, Emily's mother, leukemia was now the illness because it could kill their daughter, whereas Down syndrome was only a non-life-threatening condition. I prayed over Emily again, and in time, she was healed of the leukemia.

Emily's story reminded me of what Fr. McAlear had said once about why God allows children to have Down syndrome and autism. He said that God wanted there to be people in the world who would never commit sin. How beautiful is that? Someone who would never sin!

We have all witnessed the divine beauty of children with Down syndrome. However, many people who have babies born with Down syndrome or autism think they are being given an imperfect child. The truth is that these children reveal God's love in a way that almost no one else can. In the same way that

Fr. Cantalamessa's question and response changed the way I thought about healing, so did Emily's story. We often think of "healing" as being restored to totally perfect health. God's healing of Emily's *illness* — not the *condition* — radically changed how I viewed healing.

Emily's story also made me think about something else Fr. McAlear said about healing. He asked who is healed more — the person in a wheelchair who is full of love, mercy, and compassion, or the person who has a very strong body, can run marathons, yet is depleted by bitterness and lack of forgiveness? On the physical level, he said, the man who can run marathons is healthier, but in God's eyes, the person in the wheelchair has been healed more because he or she is full of love, mercy, and compassion.

The example of Mr. Tony Melendez comes to mind. He is the man who plays the guitar using only his feet. In 1987, Tony played "Hands in Heaven" for His Holiness, Pope John Paul II.

3

20-20 VISION

Ever since I was sixteen, I have had terrible eyesight — and because I break things easily, my glasses were always getting broken. It also didn't help that I absolutely hated wearing glasses. However, I did tend to use glasses as a screen to hide behind.

When I was at my second parish assignment, I learned how to pray as Jesus did in the story of the raising of Lazarus:

> "Father, I thank thee that thou hast heard me. I knew that thou hearest me always, but I have said this on account of the people standing by, that they may believe that thou didst send me."
>
> — JN 11:41-42

Thanking the Lord beforehand takes faith. However, that's what Jesus did when he raised Lazarus from the dead.

So I started thinking about healing and my eyesight, and I went to a bookstore to get a book about how to heal your eyes. I got an eye chart and tried figuring out all the natural ways to heal my eyes. I felt like an idiot covering one eye and trying to read the chart. Nothing worked, even after I had been doing it for half an hour. It was a lesson in futility. However, I hated glasses so much that I was willing to try to do all these things.

Also, at this time, I bought another book called, *The Power of Your Subconscious Mind*. The thesis of this book is that there are solutions in your subconscious mind that you aren't always aware of in your conscious mind. When you praise the Lord beforehand, you're setting events in motion. For example, when you get up in the morning and say, "God's going to bless me today," you're more likely to be blessed and draw blessings to yourself. If you wake up in the morning saying it's going to be a terrible day, what's going to happen? Chances are it's going to be a terrible day.

The Power of Your Subconscious Mind suggests that when you go to bed, tell your subconscious mind to lead you to what you want. I remember feeling ridiculous, but I'd say, "Subconscious mind, I command you to lead me to a place where I can get 20-20 vision." The only way I could see myself getting 20-20 vision would be through God's miraculous workings. A miracle was the only way I knew of to heal my eyesight.

At that time, I also used to go on a walk every day to try to lose a little weight. While walking, I would pray, "Thank you, Lord, for giving me 20-20 vision." I prayed it over and over again during my walks.

Two weeks later, a friend told me about a procedure called Lasik surgery. I had never heard of it, nor did I know of anyone who had ever had it. Nonetheless, I went to see the doctor in order to schedule Lasik surgery. "I don't care about the risks," I insisted. "I hate glasses so much, just sign me up."

The laser surgery would only take five minutes. Before the surgery, the doctor informed me that he would do the right eye first, then the left eye. He warned me, "Don't blink." In the middle of the surgery, with my eyelid still cut open, the doctor announced, "That went well." With that comment, I thought he was giving me permission to blink, so I blinked.

The doctor gasped. "Why did you blink?"

"Well, you said it went well," I answered. "I thought that meant I could blink." I was wrong: my eyelid was still slit, so it was the worst possible time to blink.

The doctor looked panic-stricken. He put me under a powerful microscope to try to correct the damage, and I was frightened to see the doctor panic. When he performed the surgery on the left eye, I made sure not to blink.

When my parents were driving me home after the surgery, I noticed my left eye was getting better. I could see out of my left eye, but not my right eye. At that point, I changed my prayers.

"Thank you, Jesus," I began saying, "for making my right eye more powerful than my left eye. Thank you for making the eye I blinked on more powerful than my other eye."

I had to schedule another appointment with the doctor because there could have been permanent damage to the eye as a result of my blinking. When I went back for the follow-up, my right eye was fine and stronger than my left eye. This shows how God's healing can also work through natural means.

4

DIAMONDS FROM HEAVEN

After attending a Pentecostal retreat, I went back to my parish and told the secretary, "Janet, I believe the Lord is going to give me a diamond."

She responded, "When the Lord gives you a diamond, you give me a call."

I told her, "You'll see. The Lord will give me a diamond."

Two other events happened after this. A couple days later, someone gave me four roses — three pink and a red. As many people know, St. Thérèse often sends you roses after you've made a novena to her. Here, she was sending me roses before I'd even started the novena! Needless to say, I immediately started the novena.

In the meantime, a woman named Dorothy Cotton — a woman who's like an adopted grandmother to me — called. Dorothy's thirty-seven-year-old son, Dewey, was sick with serious cancer. Although Dorothy is a Pentecostal Catholic very much baptized in the Holy Spirit, Dewey was not really much of a churchgoer. However, I gave him the Anointing of the Sick anyway. As a result, Dewey actually came back to the Church.

A few days later, I saw him and he told me that he was never going to wash the oil from his hands. Dewey actually died within the week, with the oil still on his hands.

I performed the funeral for Dewey on the ninth day of the novena, a Friday. After the funeral, Dorothy asked me if she could meet with me on Saturday. I told her that would be great.

She came to my office the next day carrying a little brown envelope. "I was praying," she explained, "and the Holy Spirit told me to give this to you." Then she set on my desk a beautiful diamond ring, a family heirloom. She was a seventy-five-year-old widow with no more family left in the world.

When I looked inside the ring, there was an engraving of a dove — the symbol of the Holy Spirit. Later, when I showed it to someone else, that person remarked, "Oh, how beautiful, a rose-cut diamond!" Of course! A rose-cut diamond would correspond to St. Thérèse's promise to present a rose as a symbol of an answered prayer.

When I received the diamond, I thought of the story of the prodigal son. The father said to put a ring on his son's finger. I thought of myself as the prodigal son, and Jesus was putting a ring on my finger.

I called Janet the next day and said, "Janet, remember how you told me to call you when the Lord gives me a diamond...?"

A few years later, while I was at another parish, I remember leaving the church one day when a woman named Sharon came up to me. She said, "Fr. Stefan, look. There's nothing on my hands."

A little puzzled, I replied, "That's very nice. There's nothing on your hands."

She said, "There are no rings on my hands," then handed me a diamond ring, and the image of Dorothy giving me the diamond ring flashed in my mind. I asked Sharon what she wanted me to do with the ring. She said I could do whatever I wanted with it.

I had already begun to pray about what I should do with the ring as I went into the church. Then, a thought came to my mind. A couple of years before, at a healing Mass, I had told a woman named Chris, "I see Jesus giving you a diamond ring. He's putting a ring on your finger." And I knew the ring was meant for her.

When I saw her I said, "Chris, remember when I said that I saw Jesus putting a ring on your finger?" She said yes, and I handed her the ring. "Well, this is the ring from Jesus. It's a gift to show you how much God loves you."

Later that night, I remember praying, "Lord, if you're giving out diamonds, I know another person who needs a diamond." I knew a young lady, sixteen or seventeen at the time, who had a problem — she was always cutting herself. I had been working with her, and she was doing remarkably better. She still, however, needed a sign of God's love and mercy, so I prayed for a ring to give to her.

The next day, a woman came up to me, took off a very beautiful and very large diamond ring, and gave it to me. I called the girl's mother and told her about the diamond I had received a couple of days earlier and the diamond I received a few years before. I told her I thought the latest one was meant for her daughter. The mother was certainly open to it. With her mother there, I gave the young lady the ring, saying, "This ring is a gift from God to show you how much he loves you."

I received about ten more rings after that. One was for a young girl for whom I had done a generational healing Mass. I gave it to her mother to give to her as another sign of God's love. I received other rings at various times — for example, when I would be hearing confessions. People would give me their rings and say, "Give this to someone who needs to be reassured of God's love." Other times, I would go into church and look down, and there'd be a little diamond lying here or there in a pew. More diamonds have come than I'd ever expected!

5

MEDJUGORJE

[NOTE: The Church's stance is that the Medjugorje apparitions are still alleged. The Church neither affirms nor denies the alleged apparitions.]

One day when I was walking across the parking lot at church, a woman I knew slightly — not even by name — came up to me and said that while she was at a recent prayer meeting, Mary, the Blessed Mother of Jesus, had told them that I, Fr. Stefan, was going to Medjugorje. She handed me an envelope containing $500 and informed me that the trip was all paid for. The $500 was meant as a deposit. I was confused how the trip could be paid for if she was handing me the deposit, but I accepted it — and the itinerary she gave me, which indicated the trip would take place in four weeks.

After looking at the travel itinerary, I called the woman in charge of the trip. I told her that I had just received money for a deposit, and I asked her if I was scheduled to go to Medjugorje in four weeks. She told me that she didn't see my name on any of the lists, but she was sure I was meant to go. A couple of hours later, she called me back. She told me I was all set. She had received another $500 to be used for my deposit, so she told me to keep the money that I had been given. She told me who had paid the additional $500 — and again, I didn't even know the person.

I learned that the story of Medjugorje began one day in 1981, when Our Lady reportedly appeared to six children in Medjugorje, Yugoslavia (Bosnia-Herzegovina). Five of the children lived in Medjugorje; one child, Mirjana, was visiting family in Medjugorje that day. The children were near a hill and saw a bright light at the top. When they investigated, they discovered that the bright light was Mary, the Mother of God.

Mary has purportedly appeared to the children as the Queen of Peace and has ten secrets to reveal to each child. Three of the children, including Mirjana, have received the tenth secret; at this point in time, the remaining three children have only received nine of the ten secrets. Once the children receive all ten secrets, Mary will continue to appear to them, but less frequently. She still appears annually to Mirjana on March 18.

Once Mary has revealed all ten secrets to all six of the children, the children have been instructed to individually contact a priest, whom they have already chosen, to reveal the secrets to the world. Then, Mary has promised to provide a sign over the town of Medjugorje to show that she has indeed been appearing there. The sign will be permanent for the whole world to see.

I was doubtful of the apparitions in Medjugorje, but I decided to go on the trip anyway, since Medjugorje is a major pilgrimage site. Millions of people who have visited Medjugorje have been converted. Millions also seek and receive the sacrament of Reconciliation there.

When I went to Medjugorje, I stayed at Mirjana's house. She is very humble and helped me to see that God was definitely doing something special there. I was the most skeptical of anyone on the trip, but Mirjana's humble example helped me overcome at least some of my skepticism.

Mirjana allowed us to ask her anything. I questioned her by saying, "Many people I know think you are making this up. What is your answer?"

She replied by saying that when the apparitions began in 1981, Yugoslavia was a Communist country where, if you talked about

God, you could lose your house and your job. The six children, who were then between the ages of six and fifteen, were interrogated by the secret police, but they never changed their story. What is the likelihood that the children would not succumb to that type of pressure?

Another convincing factor is that all the children have been given secrets, yet none of them have revealed any of them — including Ivan, one of the other visionaries, who could never keep any other secrets! When it came to these secrets from Mary, however, he said nothing.

When people think of Medjugorje, many think of it as a place where the sun spins and rosaries turn gold. I find it interesting that I experienced none of these things, especially since I have experienced so many unusual spiritual occurrences at home. However, I did witness thousands of people going to confession. Jesus says, "By their fruits you will know them."

Two experiences eventually moved me to accept that something extraordinary is happening at Medjugorje. First, I knew Mary had once appeared to me. I woke up in the middle of the night and I saw an image of Mary as Our Lady of Perpetual Help standing behind a veil. If Our Lady had appeared to me, why should I be surprised that Mary is appearing to these children? Also, many priests whom I know and respect believe in the occurrences in Medjugorje, which makes me give it more credence. However, whether or not Mary is appearing, I leave the question of Medjugorje to the judgment of the Church.

One fascinating detail about Medjugorje is that people always say that if Mary calls you there, she will protect you . . . which brings up some other interesting stories.

I was actually supposed to go to Medjugorje with a friend about ten years earlier. We were in Nice, France, and the day we were supposed to go to Medjugorje was the day that the United States accidentally bombed the Chinese Embassy in Yugoslavia. As a result of the bombing, I didn't go. My friend still went, saying that if Mary had called him there, she would protect him.

Years later, I would understand what he meant. En route to Medjugorje, we landed in Sarajevo, the epicenter of the war in Bosnia. We witnessed the incredible ruins of the war, even many years after the war was over. I was amazed that women, children, grandmothers, and grandfathers would go into this war zone with the simple trust that Mary would protect them. Our tour guide told us he had led tours throughout the war and no one has ever been hurt. Mary did protect those whom she called.

I also learned that Mary protected the town of Medjugorje as the war raged around it. No bomb ever fell on it — remarkable, in light of all the damage from the war that surrounded this little town.

6

A HOME FOR UNWED MOTHERS

When I was a young man, my parents, Florence and Paul Starzynski, were very involved in social justice; they would often take unwed mothers into their home, and I'd come home from college and find my bed occupied. My mom would reassure me that there was a bed for me behind the television. I didn't like it, but I got used to it.

In 2005, the Lord inspired me to pray about what I could do for the poor. I knew I couldn't consider myself a good Catholic — much less a good Catholic priest — if I was doing little or nothing for the poor.

At this time, I had also been praying for a couple in my parish, Randy and Evelyn, who were expecting a baby. Evelyn had been having complications during the pregnancy, and later they learned that their baby had not developed lungs. If he was carried to term, his first breath would also be his last. The doctors tried to convince them to have an abortion, but they wouldn't even consider it.

One night in October, when Evelyn was seven months pregnant, they invited me to dinner. When I arrived, Evelyn showed me an inspirational message that she had just read on a calendar that featured quotes from the *Chicken Soup* books. She had decided to go back and look at the day's message on the date that she'd had her sonogram and learned that her son would not develop lungs. That date was September 15, the feast of Our Lady of Sorrows.

The passage for that day was a poem with one line that mentioned a baby with "an amazing set of lungs," something Evelyn took to mean that the lungs of her son would be healed. I suggested that it might mean something different, but I also told her to put the poem on her refrigerator and read it every day throughout her pregnancy.

Also during her pregnancy, Evelyn and Randy came by the rectory to have me pray with them. At that time, I remember opening my Bible at random and getting a message that their baby would be born alive.

That same month, I was supposed to go on a vacation to New Jersey. However, the trip fell through. As I was talking to my pastor about where I should go — I was thinking about Montreal or maybe even the Grand Canyon — I suddenly changed my mind and thought, *No, I want to go see Our Lady of Guadalupe.* I would go to Guadalupe and pray for Evelyn and Randy's unborn baby.

I wanted my response to this inspiration to go to Guadalupe, Mexico, to be an act of faith, so I bought a ticket to travel to Mexico two days later but didn't make reservations for lodging. My plan was to tell someone on the plane that I didn't have a place to stay, and hope that they would invite me to stay with them.

However, that plan didn't exactly happen the way I envisioned it, and I arrived in Mexico with no lodging yet. About 3:00 p.m., I decided I should try to find a place to stay, so I prayed to the Blessed Mother, "Okay, Mary. You brought me here, now you have to take care of me."

A man gave me an address and told me to go there. I gave the address to a taxicab driver, and he took me to this narrow street in Mexico City and dropped me off. I went up to the house and rang the doorbell, and a nun answered the door. I don't speak any Spanish. The only Spanish words I know are "padre" and "taco." So I said to the nun, "Me Padre — no place to stay."

She responded, "You no place to stay?"

"No, me no place to stay. Let me stay here and sleep in this foyer." She brought me in and showed me to a nice little room. I said, "Thank you, Lord, for bringing me to this safe place to stay." At least I had someplace to leave my wallet and passport now.

The next morning, I woke up about 5:00 and left the house in order to spend three or four hours at the foot of the image of Our Lady of Guadalupe. This was a Monday, and everything is closed on Mondays in Guadalupe. As I was walking out of the cathedral, a man approached me and said, "Padre, do you want to go see the pyramids?"

I'd been warned about getting into unmarked taxis, about the possibility of being robbed, and the pyramids were about two hours away. So I said to the man, "If you want to rob me, I don't have my wallet or my passport. I only have about eight hundred pesos." That would amount to about eighty dollars; not much, but people have been robbed for less. But not only did I get into an unmarked car with this man, I put myself in this position to head two hours outside of the city with him. He didn't rob me — but when we returned from the pyramids, I remember going into the gift shop at the cathedral and thanking the Lord that I had made it back safely. I don't think I would ever do anything so risky again.

No sooner was I done with that prayer that a man came up to me in the gift shop and said, "I know you!" It was someone I had met while I was in Medjugorje.

"Richard!" I exclaimed. "I'm going to come visit you in about three weeks when I go to Laguna Beach." I learned he was in Guadalupe on a pilgrimage from Orange County, California. I asked him if I could join his pilgrimage and stay with him in his hotel room.

He said, "Sure." Someone else had already paid for the pilgrimage and was unable to go at the last minute. So everything — room, food, and bus tours — had been taken care of.

A few weeks later, I made that trip to Laguna Beach, California. During my trip, I started reading a book by Raymond Arroyo about Mother Angelica. In the book, I found an interesting quote from Mother Angelica. She said, "If you are willing to do the ridiculous, God will do the miraculous."

Well, I liked *that* concept. So, when I returned to Virginia, I tried to encourage the people at my parish to do the ridiculous — anything ridiculous. I saw how we were all caught up in our routines, and I was frustrated because no one was willing to step out of their comfort zone.

Meanwhile, the Lord continued to work on my heart. He kept asking me what I was doing for the poor. So I began to pray about it, choosing the St. Andrew Novena. This novena begins on the feast of St. Andrew, on November 30, and continues — with the prayer being prayed fifteen times a day! — to Christmas Day.

Confirmation day at the parish was December 4. I'd hoped the Holy Spirit would descend very powerfully upon the confirmandi, but I was rather disappointed when I didn't witness the workings of the Spirit in the way I had anticipated. So I was a little low, leaving the church that day after the Confirmation Mass — until I met two parishioners outside, Kathleen and Theresa.

As we talked, I had an idea. I asked Kathleen to pray the St. Andrew Novena with me and to ask God to give us a home for unwed mothers.

Kathleen's response? "No one will give us a home."

But I said, "You watch. Someone *will* give us a home."

About a week later, Evelyn went into labor — on December 12, the feast day of Our Lady of Guadalupe. I had brought back an image of Our Lady of Guadalupe from Mexico, and Evelyn had it in the delivery room when she gave birth.

One of the nurses, a Catholic woman named Jill, knew nothing of Evelyn and Randy's connection to Our Lady of Guadalupe or about my trip to Guadalupe. When she arrived at work that day, before going into the hospital, she opened her glove compartment and a rosary of Our Lady of Guadalupe fell into her hands. She didn't bother to put it back in the glove compartment, but slipped it into her pocket instead. And then, when Jill walked into Evelyn's room, she saw the image of Mary there.

The baby was born the day after the feast day of Our Lady of Guadalupe, and he was born without lungs. He had a very slow heartbeat, but this baby boy was never able to take a breath. Tami, the bereavement nurse, baptized, bathed, and dressed him and placed him in the arms of his parents. Evelyn and Randy were able to hold him in their arms for one hour before his little heart stopped beating.

I remember being called to the hospital. Out of gratitude for everything I had done, Evelyn and Randy named the baby after me and another priest they admired, Fr. Paul Scalia. The baby was named Paul Stefan. (Interestingly, my name is Stefan Paul Starzynski; my confirmation name is Paul.)

In February of the next year, I went on a trip to Israel for nine days — just the amount of time needed for a novena. Every day of my trip, I offered Masses for two intentions: for the release of the Holy Spirit, and that God would give me a home for unwed mothers.

The first place I went to in Israel was Elijah's Cave. The story of Elijah in the cave relates that God wasn't in the wind, he wasn't in the storm, and he wasn't in the earthquake. There was a still, small voice, and Elijah hid his face because God was in that still, small voice (see 1 Kings 19:11-13). I heard the still, small voice in Elijah's Cave. God wanted me to receive homes for unwed mothers.

After completing the novena and my trip, I returned home and celebrated a Mass and healing service. While I was at the pulpit, I related how I had heard God in Israel, in Elijah's Cave, speaking to me in a still, small voice. I said that the homes already existed; we just needed to step into them.

I also announced that there were five people present there that night who were meant to give me $1,000 each. The importance was not in the money itself, but the act of giving would be an act of faith on the part of the donors in responding to God's call. I received the $5,000 that night — five checks written out to me. I thought, *Okay, what do I do now?* Had I acted rashly in a moment of exuberance?

What I didn't know then was that before the birth and death of their son, Randy and Evelyn had decided to immerse themselves in the pro-life movement. When they heard about my prayers to start a home for unwed mothers, they felt called to become a part of it. Thus, we scheduled our first meeting of cofounding members and appointed Randy as president. Randy was instrumental in setting up the Paul Stefan Foundation. At first, he thought God was calling him to sell property he owned in Orange, Virginia; he would use the profit from this sale to build a home. But, amazingly, God had other plans.

The day after I received the $5,000, a woman approached me whose husband works for a gas company that has a pipeline extending from San Antonio to New York City. About twenty miles down the road from the parish, the gas company owned two houses and seventy acres of land. There were plans to demolish the homes. When she heard my homily, she decided to talk to her husband to see if the gas company could provide the houses as homes for unwed mothers.

The first time I visited one of the houses, I found "a rose" in the house — an artificial rose, but a rose nonetheless — and said, *Thank you, St. Thérèse.* Today, I still display that rose in my office. I also found a Bible, so I prayed to Jesus that when I opened the Bible at random, he would give me a message regarding the future of the Paul Stefan Home. When I opened the Bible, I saw Isaiah 57:13: "He who takes refuge in me shall possess the land and shall inherit my holy mountain."

In my mind, it was all set. However, the decision to allow the Paul Stefan Foundation to occupy the homes had to be made by the CEO of the company. We spent most of the Lent of 2006 waiting for the decision and finally received word that we were to be given the houses to lease for one dollar a year.

In honor of baby Paul Stefan and God's loving provision, we decided to name the homes for expectant mothers the Paul Stefan Home of Our Lady of Guadalupe. The Lord had answered our prayers to give us a home for unwed mothers and had woven it together with the beautiful story of the life and death of Paul Stefan. Although Paul Stefan lived for only an hour, his little lungs were and are filled with the Holy Spirit, and they proclaim that every life is precious.

When we received the houses, we understood the meaning of the poem from September 15. The poem had mentioned a baby with an amazing set of lungs. If Paul Stefan had lived, his lungs would have been like any other baby's lungs. But in death, through the Paul Stefan Homes for Expectant Mothers, Paul Stefan has an amazing set of lungs, allowing him to spread the word about the Home around the world.

During the summer of 2006, I experienced a lot of fear and anxiety about whether God had, in fact, called me to do this, and how it would succeed. It certainly appeared that the devil didn't want that to happen! We encountered many difficulties and problems. Egos got in the way, causing misunderstandings between people, and I was trying my best to make everyone happy. I thought about abandoning the project, but I felt that if I left, the project would fail. However, through all this, God kept saying, "Trust in me despite all your fears."

That summer, I traveled to Germany to visit Megan, who is like a sister to me. She came to live with my family when she became pregnant while attending a large Catholic high school in Northern Virginia. After giving birth, Megan gave the baby up for adoption, but she continued to live with my family for a couple of years. Megan eventually graduated from college and got married. She and her husband moved to Germany.

The day I arrived, Megan picked me up at the airport, and we went to a little coffee shop in Frankfurt. As we were drinking our coffee and eating our pastries, Megan said to me, "Stefan, if it was not for your mother and father, I would have had no place to go."

Her social worker wasn't able to find a place for her to stay. It was then that I realized how few homes there are for unwed mothers. I also realized that if a woman has an abortion because she has no place to go, then we as a Church are partly responsible. Yes, we are our brothers' (and sisters') keeper.

During the trip to Germany, Megan and I drove to Paray-le-Monial in southern France, where Jesus revealed his Sacred Heart to St. Margaret Mary. We stayed in a hotel right across the street from the church; I could see the church from my window. I woke up with a perfect Scripture passage, but at the time I didn't even realize that it was from Scripture, for I was unfamiliar with the verse:

> And he [Jesus] said, "The kingdom of God is as if a man should scatter seed upon the ground, and should sleep and rise night and day, and the seed should sprout and grow, he knows not how."
>
> — MK 4:26-27

What a perfect Scripture to help me with my anxiety and fear. I am the farmer. I plant the seed, but it is up to Jesus to make it grow. How it grows he (Fr. Stefan) knows not how. The Paul Stefan Home doesn't depend on me. Jesus is the one who will make it grow, and grow in a way I know not how.

Our first house opened on September 10, 2006. We've had more than a dozen women live there thus far. Our first mother at the home came from a homeless shelter. She went into labor on the feast day of Our Lady of Guadalupe, exactly one year to the day after Evelyn went into labor with Paul Stefan. The mother gave birth the next day, on the anniversary of Paul Stefan's birth and death. It was confirmation for me that we had followed God's plan. The baby was named Andrew. This was also a welcome confirmation, since the prayer that started the quest to do something "ridiculous" for God started with a novena to St. Andrew.

The Paul Stefan Home has also placed our first adoption. A kindergarten teacher and her husband were not able to have children. They love children, and to be unable to have children was a difficult cross for them. They were teaching an Engaged Encounter one day, and I was the chaplain for the retreat. In my homily at Mass for the engaged couples, I announced to everyone that they would be the first to adopt a baby from the Paul Stefan Home. This was prophecy because at the time, I had no knowledge of a mother who wished to place her baby for adoption.

However, there was a woman staying at the Paul Stefan Home who had met and liked them. Later, they would adopt her baby, the first baby from the home. A few weeks after the adoption, I had the honor of baptizing baby Paul.

Our second home opened on April 20, 2008. The first home is for women who are pregnant. The second home is for women who have already had their babies and need a place to stay.

I celebrated the first Mass at the house before any women moved in. The reading that day was from the book of Isaiah: "They shall call you, 'Restorer of ruined homesteads'" (Is 58:12, NAB). What a perfect image of repairing these old farmhouses. It struck me that this was not about two houses. This was about hundreds, if not thousands, of homes. God wants to create many homes for unwed mothers. It occurred to me that we may be only five to ten years away from the end of *Roe v. Wade*. If *Roe v. Wade* will be overturned, doesn't it make sense that God would anticipate all this by creating homes for unwed mothers? If you're willing to do the ridiculous, God will do the miraculous.

I relate the overturning of *Roe v. Wade* to the fall of the Berlin Wall. In the 1980s, it looked like the Berlin Wall would never fall. Then, one day in 1989, unexpectedly the wall came down. The same will happen with *Roe v. Wade*. We're going to wake up one morning and find out that *Roe v. Wade* has been overturned. We will have to have already created homes nationwide. The Paul Stefan Homes of Our Lady of Guadalupe will be waiting to welcome pregnant women and single mothers across the nation.

7

THE LITTLE FLOWER

My first encounter with St. Thérèse of Lisieux, also known as the Little Flower, was at a retirement home for priests. I toured the retirement home one day, and the woman giving the tour showed us a display case containing dozens of roses. They were roses that had been given to the priests at the home.

She explained to me that when St. Thérèse answers your prayers, she gives you a rose. I remember thinking, *How beautiful*. St. Thérèse promised that after her death, she would cause a shower of roses to fall from heaven.

Since I first learned about St. Thérèse, I have loved her. I have always felt like I have a sister in heaven. Maybe it's because she was so simple. She was a simple girl, filled with the love of God, who yearned to convert the entire world. Her courage and faith inspired me to love her. I also love her because Thérèse felt it was her vocation to pray for priests. I have always felt that I am in great need of prayer, and beloved St. Thérèse is in heaven praying for me and all priests.

St. Thérèse is the third female doctor of the Church. She taught the doctrine of spiritual childhood — the way of trust and absolute self-surrender to God.

St. Thérèse desired to preach on every continent, in every nation in the world. I remember the day, October 19, 1997, when

St. Thérèse was declared a Doctor of the Church. Her body was on display at the National Shrine of the Immaculate Conception in Washington, DC. I had to celebrate the 12:10 p.m. Mass at St. Mary's Church in Alexandria that day, and the Mass at the shrine for St. Thérèse was at 1:00 p.m.

The entire shrine was full of the faithful by 11:00 that morning. When I arrived around 2:00 p.m., there were no parking spaces available. As I drove around looking for a place to park, I thought to myself, *Fr. McAlear teaches right across the street from the shrine at the seminary, The Oblates of Mary Immaculate.* I drove over to the seminary, and there was one parking space. I parked and went into the shrine. The Mass was over, and they were about to begin the veneration of her body. I worked my way into the first pew, and had the honor of venerating her body. I remember thinking how nice it would be to concelebrate the Mass with her body present.

Five months later, I went on vacation with my friend Fr. Paul to Seattle, Washington. Before the trip, he mentioned to me that the day we were scheduled to arrive in Seattle was the same day that St. Thérèse's body would be in the cathedral there. The next day, I had the honor of concelebrating the Mass at the cathedral with her body present.

After I had gone to the National Shrine of the Immaculate Conception the day St. Thérèse was declared a Doctor of the Church, I started praying a novena to her for the healing of a relationship. By the time I arrived in Seattle, the relationship had been healed.

Wednesday during Holy Week, I went to a detention center in Virginia. Although it was Wednesday, I was actually going to offer the Good Friday service, where people kiss the wood of the Cross.

I told the inmates the story about how St. Thérèse, the Little Flower, had once read about a man named Pranzini who was on death row. Pranzini had turned his back on help from God or clergy. Thérèse prayed for his conversion and asked God to give her a sign when it happened. She trusted that God would show her the sign.

From all outward appearances, there was nothing that Pranzini did as he waited on death row that indicated that he was looking for a conversion. However, Thérèse had faith in the mercy of God. I related to the prisoners that on the day of his execution, Pranzini took the cross and kissed the feet of Jesus three times before he went to the guillotine. Thérèse accepted this as the sign that Pranzini was converted.

After I told this story to the inmates, some who had committed felonies or serious crimes, and some who had committed misdemeanors, less serious crimes, I asked them, "Where do you think he went? He embraced God's mercy, and he went to heaven."

At that moment, I held up the cross we venerate on Good Friday. Every inmate came forward and kissed the feet of Jesus in such a beautiful manner, every inmate trusting in God's mercy.

After that, something extraordinary happened. Grace filled that gym in the detention center. As I was walking toward the door, a man stopped me and asked me if he could go to confession. Then a woman asked. Then, suddenly Catholics and non-Catholics were all confessing their sins to me. They were all looking for God's mercy.

This story of St. Thérèse , the Little Flower, that I related to the inmates provided the means for abundant conversions. I remember the guard saying he had never witnessed anything like this before. St. Thérèse obtained these conversions, and they are examples of mercy touching the hearts of all these people, turning their hearts of stone into hearts of flesh.

In May of 2008, I did a funeral for a woman named Joan. Eight days before she passed away, knowing that she only had days to live, this sixty-one-year-old Methodist cancer patient told her husband that she wanted to become Catholic.

My current pastor went to her home and confirmed her. She chose Joan of Arc as her confirmation saint. Joan also received First Holy Communion that day, along with Anointing of the Sick, as she was brought into the Catholic Church.

While I was meeting with Joan's husband in my office discussing funeral arrangements, he looked at the picture of St. Thérèse hanging in my office and was intrigued by it; he asked me to tell him about her. I told him how St. Thérèse gave the Church the "Little Way." I explained that God doesn't look at how big our actions are, but rather He looks at the love that drives our actions.

I also shared with him how when St. Thérèse answers our prayers, she gives us roses. He thought this was very interesting. In his backyard, he said, a rose bush appeared with twelve perfect roses eight days before Joan died. It was when the rosebush appeared that Joan decided to become Catholic. He said he was intrigued by the roses. I told him, "It looks like St. Thérèse obtained the grace for your wife, Joan, to receive the Eucharist right before she died."

Her husband asked me if I had any books he could borrow about St. Thérèse, and I handed him two of mine. Then something remarkable occurred to me; as he was leaving the church, I caught up with him and told him to look at the cover of one of the books. The picture on the cover was St. Thérèse dressed as her favorite saint, Joan of Arc.

8

GOD'S DIVINE MERCY

The first assignment I had while I was in the seminary was to go to Boys Town with Fr. Terry. We drove from Washington, DC, all the way to Nebraska in his car — which, incidentally, was on its last leg. We couldn't travel over fifty-five miles per hour the entire trip. After about sixteen hours in the car, we made it to Iowa and exclaimed, "Oh, thank the Lord! We're only one state away." We didn't realize that one state away still meant seven more hours of driving!

My job at Boys Town that summer was to take care of the boys who had just arrived off the streets. I had to teach these boys to clean the pigs. It was a very difficult and messy task. Like the boys, I was always getting covered in slop and guck. I even went to Fr. Val Peter, the head person at Boys Town, and said, "Fr. Peter, I quit! I can't do this!"

He replied that if I quit Boys Town, he thought I would also quit the seminary. So, I didn't quit — but he did give me two weeks off.

During my time off, I came across the diary of Sister Faustina, now known as St. Faustina. God's revelation of His infinite mercy, as told to Sister Faustina, filled me with awe. In the diary, I immediately saw a connection between Jesus' revelation to St. Margaret Mary Alacoque in the seventeenth century and his revelation to Sister Faustina in the twentieth century. Jesus had said to St.

Margaret Mary, "This is my heart which has so loved man but has received from him nothing but ingratitude."

In the diary of Sister Faustina, Jesus speaks of his overwhelming desire to love man and grant him mercy. The Lord freely and limitlessly pours out his mercy upon mankind. This revelation of the love of God that the greater the sinner, the greater the right to receive God's mercy, profoundly moved me. This was my first encounter with Sister Faustina's diary, and it was so compelling that I read the entire book in a week.

After my two weeks off, I returned to work on the farm at Boys Town. This was the summer of 1993, during the great floods in the Midwest. When the flooding occurred, our work schedule changed; we were able to get more counselors to help with the boys, and we were able to do different jobs. My new job was easier, and I could rely on other people for help. The floods were probably instrumental in saving my vocation, because I don't know if I could have done the work and handled the boys otherwise.

Fr. Ron Pytel was the pastor of Holy Rosary Parish in Baltimore, Maryland, a parish centered on the Divine Mercy Devotion.

Fr. Ron had a very serious heart condition. He described it to me in this way. The number for a healthy heart of an eighteen-year-old marathon runner is 65. If your number is 15, you're dead. Fr. Ron's number was 20.

Fr. Ron underwent heart catheterization surgery in June 1995. In August, while he was still recovering, his parishioners went on a pilgrimage to the tomb of Blessed Faustina in Warsaw, Poland, to pray for him. At the same time, Fr. Ron also participated in Divine Mercy devotions at his church. Then, on October 5, 1995, the anniversary of Blessed Faustina's death, some of his parishioners came together to pray for his healing through her intercession. Fr. Ron was blessed by a first-class relic (a piece of bone or hair) of Blessed Faustina; when the relic touched him, he fell to the ground. A woman told him, "I want you to know that Blessed Faustina is obtaining your healing right now."

A month later, Fr. Ron went back to the doctor for his scheduled appointment. After looking at the results of his echocardiogram, the doctor told him his heart was normal. The number for his heart had been 20, and now the number was 70. Remember, the number for a healthy eighteen- year-old marathon runner's heart is 65!

One of Fr. Ron's friends, Fr. Larry Gesy, decided that they should take this case of healing through the intercession of Blessed Faustina to be used as the second miracle needed for her canonization. I thought, "Oh, right. You don't really think that could happen." But when it was given to Cardinal Keeler of Baltimore, that was exactly what did happen.

Fr. Ron's cardiologist traveled to Rome and testified that he had never witnessed healing of this type, and that heart damage does not reverse itself. The devil's advocates — the people who try to disprove the miracle — said that his heart could get better with medicine and exercise. The doctor agreed that yes, it could get better; the numbers could go from 20 to 22, 23, maybe even 24 or 25. But Fr. Ron's numbers went from 20 to 70.

Fr. Ron's healing was proven to be a miracle, and it was used for the canonization of Blessed Faustina. She was canonized as St. Faustina on Divine Mercy Sunday, the Sunday after Easter, in the year 2000. She was also the first saint to be canonized in the new millennium by John Paul II. John Paul II said that the twenty-first century will be an age of mercy or it won't be an age at all.

I remember Fr. Ron's reflection on why it was his heart that was damaged and subsequently healed. He said it was his heart because the heart is the seat of mercy.

Fr. Gesy also gave me a first-class relic of St. Faustina, which is one of my most prized possessions.

In the year 2000, a young student asked me if I would meet with him — a surprise, because teenagers do not usually want to meet with priests. When I met with him, I discovered he was a very troubled young man. I told him I would give him my relic of St. Faustina if he promised to look at it every single day. I told him how important the relic was to me and how much I treasured it. He assured me that he would look at it every day. Because it was so important to me, it also became very important to him as well.

Six years later, during Divine Mercy Week (which I recognized as a divine coincidence), I got a phone call from a woman.

"Fr. Stefan," she said, "do you remember Jacob?" I thought for a moment, but I couldn't recall Jacob. Then she mentioned the relic of St. Faustina, and I remembered him. But what she told me next shocked me: Jacob had committed suicide the night before.

She told me that he had the relic with him when he died, and it was his most cherished possession. He even used to tell his mother that the relic was more important to him than his sister.

When I prepared to do the funeral, I found out that Jacob had continued to be a very troubled youth. He had been kicked out of school. However, despite all his trouble, he was always a very good boy, but Jacob didn't see himself as a very good boy. In fact, he had never received the Sacrament of Confirmation because he hadn't felt that he was worthy of the sacrament.

At the funeral, I met many of the friends Jacob had hung out with. They were a cross-section of some of the most troubled young people that I had met in Alexandria and DC — drug addicts, prostitutes, and the like. I learned from Jacob's friends what a good person he had been. One thing Jacob had done, for anyone who asked, was to give them the relic, telling them to keep it for their protection. The relic had been held by homeless men and women, prostitutes, and drug addicts all over the DC metro area, but it had always come back to him. His friends also told me that Jacob had told everyone he met about me. This surprised me.

As we went through the funeral service, I remember thinking, "This is what it should be like. The Church is a place of healing, and Jesus said he came to call the tax collectors and the prostitutes"(see Mk 2:16-17).

After I gave the relic to Jacob six years earlier, I visited Fr. Kosicki, the head of the Divine Mercy Shrine in Stockbridge, Massachusetts, to ask him if I could have another relic. He asked me what I did with the first one. When I told him I had given it away, he said, "You fool! Why would you give it away? Don't you know how impossible these are to obtain?" But that hadn't been part of my thought process at the time; I'd given Jacob the relic because I knew it would help him trust in God's mercy.

On the day of the funeral, Jacob's mother said she wanted to return the relic to me, but I didn't want to take it — I told her I wanted the relic to go in the coffin with Jacob. However, she insisted that I take it back, that Jacob would want me to have it. When I accepted it, I remember thinking that there'll probably be another Jacob somewhere who will need it.

I thought about how important this relic was to Jacob. He prized it because I prized it. Although Jacob died a tragic death, he received God's mercy. I had extended mercy to Jacob through the gift of St. Faustina's relic, and mercy returned to me when the relic returned to me. The circle of mercy was complete.

––––––––––

The week after Easter in 2005, I took a trip to San Diego to visit a friend. On the way to the airport for my flight home, I told my friend that I had had a great time, but I didn't feel like I had quite had my "adventure" for the week yet.

I had been in a lot of pain that day, pain of a type that I'd never experienced before, and I had no idea what was causing it. (I would later learn that I had gout.) The pain was so excruciating that I could barely move. Slowly, I limped through the airport that night in order to catch my 10:30 flight back to Washington, DC.

As luck would have it, my flight was delayed. We eventually boarded the plane, about 11:00 or 11:30 p.m., then all just sat there with no indication that the plane would take off anytime soon. Finally, just as the plane did taxi down the runway, all the computers went dead. It was now about 12:30 in the morning, and the plane returned to the terminal. By this time the San Diego Airport was closed; it closes from midnight until 5:00 am.

It was now Saturday, the Saturday before Divine Mercy Sunday. I always pray the Divine Mercy Novena, which begins on Good Friday and continues through the Saturday before Divine Mercy Sunday. As I hopped through the airport on one foot, I thought, *It's Saturday. I might as well pray the prayers for the ninth day of the novena.* At the end of the novena, the prayer is, "In difficult moments might we not despair nor become despondent, but with great confidence submit ourselves to Your holy will, which is Love and Mercy itself."

As I was praying this prayer, a young girl came up to me and said, "Fr. Stefan, I thought that was you. My mother also thought it was you." She was a student from one of my previous parishes. She was traveling with her parents and both of her grandmothers. In a beautiful "coincidence," both of the grandmothers were also praying the Divine Mercy Novena, so the three of us sat there and prayed the ninth-day prayers together.

The family was traveling on the same DC-bound flight as I was, so I said to the father, a colonel, "There are no longer five in your family. I'm now an official member of your family." I thought, being a colonel, he was very smart and would figure out a way to get us on a flight home.

At first, things didn't look good. At that point, an airline agent working at the counter relayed the bad news: because it was beach week, there were no more flights out of San Diego until Tuesday. Everyone was frustrated, and some passengers began yelling, but I just sat there quietly; I couldn't move because of the gout.

But then, at about 1:30 a.m., the colonel approached the agent at the counter and said to her, "You may not know to do this, but

I'd like you to check for seats on Alaskan Air." In San Diego, *I* certainly don't think of traveling by Alaskan Air, but as it turns out, Alaskan Air has one terminal in DC. *This is why he's a colonel*, I thought. *He analyzes a situation and then takes the appropriate steps to resolve it.*

So the agent checked, and — clearly surprised — said, "Oh my gosh, you're right! There are five seats on Alaskan Air from here to Chicago, and Chicago to Washington tomorrow at 9:00 a.m." That took care of the family, and I had to be happy for them.

Then I asked the agent, "What about me? Is there another seat on Alaskan Air?" When she checked, there was one seat available on a flight from San Diego to Seattle, and Seattle to Washington, DC.

As the agent and I talked, I happened to say, "Wouldn't it be beautiful if John Paul II died on Divine Mercy Sunday?" We must have both been thinking that, because when I brought it up, the agent told me she also been praying the Divine Mercy novena! So, right there at the counter, we both prayed the ninth day of the novena together. We focused on the words, "In difficult moments might we not despair nor become despondent, but with great confidence submit ourselves to Your holy will, which is Love and Mercy itself." We both agreed that it would be beautiful if John Paul II died on Divine Mercy Sunday.

That night, I slept on a chair in the food court. I wasn't wearing my clerics, but I even celebrated Mass in the food court the next morning, on a table in front of McDonald's. It was probably the only time Mass had ever been celebrated in the food court in the San Diego airport.

As I was flying to Seattle that day, I saw the news report that John Paul II had died a couple of hours earlier. What we had talked about had come to pass. John Paul II had passed away on Divine Mercy Sunday.

Jesus had said to St. Faustina that honoring Divine Mercy Sunday is the last chance for mercy for all of humanity, and one privilege that I've had as a priest is that of participating in and encouraging Divine Mercy devotion in every parish to which I've been assigned. I've even started Divine Mercy Sunday devotions in two of them.

How did the Divine Mercy devotion start?

On October 5, 1938, a young religious by the name Sr. Faustina (Helen Kowalska) died in a convent of the Congregation of Sisters of Our Lady of Mercy in Cracow, Poland. She had come from a very poor family that had struggled hard on their little farm during the terrible years of World War I, and Sister had received only three years of very simple education. Hers were the humblest of tasks in the convent, usually in the kitchen or the vegetable garden, or as a porter.

But on February 22, 1931, Our Lord and Savior Jesus Christ appeared to this simple nun, bringing with him a wonderful message of mercy for all mankind. St. Faustina tells us in her diary under this date:

> In the evening, when I was in my cell, I became aware of the Lord Jesus clothed in a white garment. One hand was raised in blessing; the other was touching the garment at the breast. From the opening of the garment at the breast there came forth two large rays, one red and the other pale. In silence I gazed intently at the Lord; my soul was overwhelmed with fear, but also with great joy. After a while Jesus said to me, "Paint an image according to the pattern you see, with the inscription: 'Jesus, I trust in You.'"
>
> — *DIARY*, #47

The following day, an inner voice taught her to say this prayer on ordinary rosary beads:

Begin by saying one Our Father, one Hail Mary, and the Apostles' Creed. Then, on the large beads say the following words: *Eternal Father, I offer You the Body and Blood, Soul and Divinity of Your dearly beloved Son, Our Lord Jesus Christ, in atonement for our sins and those of the whole world.*

On the smaller beads, you are to say the following words: *For the sake of His sorrowful Passion, have mercy on us and on the whole world.*

In conclusion, you are to say these words three times: *Holy God, Holy Mighty One, Holy Immortal One, have mercy on us and on the whole world.*

That is the Divine Mercy chaplet, and it can be said anytime, anywhere — even stranded in an airport! — to help remind us of the eternal mercy of the Lord.

9

A GHOST IN MY ROOM

One night, I was lying on my bed in my room, in that twilight stage of not completely asleep, nor fully awake. When I looked toward my right, I saw a "man" whose body had no substance. He was a man, though, with a bald head and a very thin face. There were buttons going down the front of his cassock. He looked like a priest from a hundred years ago, and not at all frightening; I wasn't afraid when I saw him. In fact, afterward, I just went to sleep.

The next morning, I told my mom I had seen a ghost in my room. I described the vision as chalk on black paper. Even though I saw him for only a moment, I remembered his characteristics very clearly. I just didn't know who the man was. And I didn't find out until two years later, when an acquaintance went to the church of Our Lady of Victory in Lackawanna, New York. When she came back, she showed me a picture of Fr. Nelson Baker, and I recognized him as the ghost who had appeared in my bedroom!

I then remembered that as a young child, I had heard my aunt, a nun in Buffalo, speak of Fr. Baker. She had once pointed out that the house at the end of the driveway was a "Fr. Baker House." This was the only knowledge I had of him.

Fr. Baker's calling was helping abandoned boys and unwed mothers. (When he had appeared in my room, it was still a few years before my initial thoughts of creating the Paul Stefan Home.)

According to an article in the Buffalo *Times*, during his ministry, Fr. Baker fed 50 million meals to the hungry. During the Great Depression, he served more than a million meals per year. He gave away millions of loaves of bread and clothed half a million people. He gave medical care to 250,000 and supplied medicine to 200,000 more. Over 300,000 men, women, and children received some sort of training at his hands. A hundred thousand boys were trained for trades. Six hundred unmarried mothers in their distress knocked at his door and did not knock in vain. Because of Fr. Baker, more than 6,000 destitute and abandoned babies were placed in foster homes. At Fr. Baker's funeral in 1936, Lackawanna's streets were flooded with almost half a million people he had saved, physically and spiritually, or whose parents or grandparents he had saved.

After Fr. Baker's apparition and after learning who he was, I felt called to go on a retreat at the church he created in honor of Our Lady of Victory, where his body is now located. Fr. Baker was calling me to visit to his church, as if he had chosen me to continue his work.

Since I have come to know Fr. Baker, I have fallen in love with him. Here was a man who was willing to do the ridiculous so that God could do the miraculous. He saw many needs, such as the need for a place for abandoned boys and unwed mothers and their babies. He trusted that God would help him to help people in need. When you look at the millions of people he helped, it shows how God can use one person to affect the lives of so many.

Fr. Baker knew that God would lead me to open a home for unwed mothers. That is the reason why he appeared to me: I was to continue his work under the guidance of his prayers for me.

Before I left to visit the Shrine of Our Lady of Victory in early June 2008, I asked my congregation to give me their petitions so I could pray for their intentions at the tomb of Fr. Baker. I asked them how many of them believed that one of their petitions could be the miracle needed to make Fr. Baker a Blessed in the Catholic Church, and a few people in the church raised their hands.

For those who might be unfamiliar with the terms "blessed" and "saint," here's a short explanation. When the Vatican believes that a deceased person showed signs of holiness during their lifetime, a case may be opened and the person declared a Servant of God. Right now, Fr. Baker is a Servant of God. In order to declare Fr. Baker as Blessed, the Church needs a miracle attributed to his intercession. In order to become a saint, the beatified person then needs verification of a second miracle attributed to them. When one becomes a "blessed" or a saint, the Church allows the veneration of the person to be more extensive. The Church holds the person up as a model of holiness and encourages the faithful to learn about them and seek their intercession.

While I was visiting Our Lady of Victory, I told Msgr. Paul Burkard, the pastor, how Fr. Baker had appeared to me. He replied that Fr. Baker was certainly getting around; Msgr. Burkard had received similar reports of Fr. Baker's appearances from all over the world. I asked him then if I could have a relic of Fr. Baker.

I spent eight hours praying before Fr. Baker's tomb that day, witnessing the beautiful faith of the people who came to pray there. While I was praying, I asked Fr. Baker to please give me a relic as a sign that I was supposed to be there. He did; I met a woman who had been a seamstress to Fr. Baker. She still had a large piece of his vestments, so she placed seven pieces of his vestments in seven holy cards and laminated them for me. Also, before I left, Msgr. Burkard took two relics from the rectory which had been used to bless people and gave them to me.

When I told my mom that I was going to Our Lady of Victory Church to visit the tomb of Fr. Baker, she told me that she used to take me there when I was a young boy. My mom is from Buffalo. I believe that Fr. Baker looked down on me from heaven when I was little and said, "I want this boy to continue my work."

I left Our Lady of Victory Church on June 6, 2008. While sitting in the Buffalo airport, I started talking to a woman who told me her name was Debbie, and that she was a professional singer who had just finished a show in Toronto, Canada. Debbie had a critical form of cancer and had been given only a few months to live, so her husband was encouraging her to do all the things she wanted to do before she died.

I told her about Fr. Baker and my visit to Our Lady of Victory Church and gave her a picture of him, along with a relic of his vestment. Then I prayed over her through Fr. Baker's intercession.

Afterward, I didn't think much about my meeting with Debbie until, some time later, a parishioner told me that the woman I prayed for in Buffalo was healed. It seemed that this parishioner had a friend who was also a professional singer. This singer knew Debbie, the same Debbie for whom I had prayed in the Buffalo airport. Now, Debbie and I had not exchanged any contact information when we met — God used his servants as contacts to relay the information to me and to her.

A couple of days later, Debbie called me on the phone and told me the good news herself. She told me that she had suffered from Stage 4 metastasis melanoma, a cancer that is the second most aggressive form of the disease, second only to pancreatic cancer. A diagnosis of Stage 4 metastasis melanoma is a death sentence.

Over the phone, she told me the course of events. I had met her on June 6th at the airport. That is when I said to her, "Let us trust that Fr. Baker will intercede for you and this will be the miracle he needs in order to be beatified." I gave her the picture and a piece of his vestment. She told me that one week later, two women came up to her and started talking about healing. One of the women said, "You ought to go to Fr. Stefan's Healing Mass."

Debbie said, "Fr. Stefan? That is the priest who prayed over me in the Buffalo airport."

The two ladies said, "Do you believe that when he prayed for you, you were healed?"

She said, "Yes, I do believe that I was healed." (And later, she learned that she was!)

So as we talked, I asked, "Would you help me gather the medical evidence for your healing? I think this is the miracle that Fr. Baker needs to make him Blessed." She said that she would be honored to do whatever was necessary. When I spoke with her a week or so later, she confirmed that she was gathering the medical evidence we needed for the miracle to be attributed to the intercession of Fr. Baker.

The next day, in my excitement, I went to the Arlington Diocese office of Bishop Paul S. Loverde unannounced. The bishop listened attentively to my story with great faith and love. What I didn't know was that Bishop Loverde was familiar with the legacy of Fr. Baker, and he personally knew Msgr. Burkard, the rector at the Fr. Baker Shrine.

The first thing he said to me was that he thought Fr. Baker should have been canonized a long time ago. He said it had been his prayer for many years that Fr. Baker would become a saint.

Bishop Loverde told me he would talk to Msgr. Burkard the following week, while he was in Buffalo for a retreat. The bishop then asked me for a framed picture of Fr. Baker, gave me a big hug, and left me with the encouraging words, "Fr. Stefan, you are a good and faithful priest."

As of this writing, we are pursuing Fr. Baker's cause for sainthood. The Lord has his ways, and it seems that this miracle could be the one that Fr. Baker needs to be beatified.

10

ANGELS, MUSTARD SEEDS, AND HEALINGS OF CANCER

I was sleeping in my room one night when an angel came to me. I couldn't see the angel, but I knew the angel was there. Actually, it was more than an angel; it was the holiness of God. When it happened, I was immediately moved from lying on my bed to being on my knees. It would have been impossible to just lie there in the presence of the Holy!

St. John of the Cross says that the most authentic touches of God are intellectual visitations. God does not touch the sense, but he touches the soul directly. In these visitations, you may not see anything, but you know intellectually that you have been touched by an angel or a saint.

The angel had a message for me that I remember to this day. I can honestly say I had no idea how this message could come true, "but with God, all things are possible" (Mt 19:26). Although I will not reveal the message here, I know the message I received is coming true.

This experience reminded me of when an angel visited Isaiah and put a coal on his lips. Isaiah said, "I am a man of unclean lips, and I dwell in the midst of a people of unclean lips; for my eyes have seen the King, the LORD of hosts" (Is 6:5). It also reminded me of a book I read by a man named Rudolf Otto. According to this book *The Idea of the Holy,* this holiness is not primarily ethical — i.e., living righteously — but primarily about the awesomeness of God. To encounter the holy is to encounter the awesomeness, or *oth-*erness, of God in relation to ourselves. The angels say God is "Holy, Holy, Holy" because God is totally separate from us.

Otto says that if we experience the holiness of God, we know it. If there is any doubt, we have not experienced the holiness of God. One sign that we have experienced God's holiness is dread, such as Isaiah had when he experienced the angel. According to Otto, experiencing the Holy is akin to seeing a ghost and having all your hair stand on end. Upon seeing the angel and receiving the message, I experienced the holiness of God as Otto describes it.

I am not entirely sure yet what my visitation by the angel means, but I pray that I may have the courage to say to the Lord with Isaiah, "Here I am! Send me" (Is 6:8).

———

One evening, visiting the children's religious instruction classes, I came into one room where everyone had a mustard seed. The mustard seed is the smallest of all seeds, but if you have faith like a mustard seed, Jesus said you can move mountains (see Mt 17:20).

I took one of the mustard seeds to another classroom, where Iris was teaching her class. I knew that Iris couldn't eat any wheat or dairy products. I handed her the mustard seed and said, "I think God wants you to try to eat some dairy and wheat."

A few days later, Iris came up to me after Mass and said that she had started eating dairy and wheat again for the first time in twelve years. It was a little miracle, but a great miracle. Iris's miracle shows us how God can touch us and heal us.

> "If you have faith as a grain of mustard seed, you will say to this mountain, 'Move hence to yonder place,' and it will move; and nothing will be impossible to you."
>
> — Mt 17:20

Margaret had cancer, so she came to see me for the Anointing of the Sick. A couple of days later, Margaret came back and told me that the cancer was completely healed.

Interestingly enough, even as this miracle was occurring during the anointing, I remember feeling dry, as if nothing was happening. However, God is amazing. Even when you don't feel like anything is happening and don't expect it, miracles occur. I realized that we can't always gauge God's workings by how we feel.

Another person who has been healed of cancer is Kathy, a religious education teacher. She came to my monthly Mass and healing service and I prayed over her. This time, too, as with Margaret, I didn't expect anything because I hadn't felt anything when I prayed for her. However, she, too, was healed. It is absolutely beautiful how the Lord works through us, even when we may not "feel" it.

In April 2007, I decided to go on a little vacation. Again, I chose a spot at random. This time it was Montreal. I had always wanted to go to Montreal to see the beautiful church, St. Joseph's Oratory, which was built by Blessed Andre Bessette in the early twentieth century. He was a religious brother of the Congregation of the Holy Cross who was assigned to the duty of porter at Notre-Dame College in Montreal. This humble brother received people at his post and, with simple faith, healed thousands of them by trusting in the Lord and praying to St. Joseph.

In addition to his healing ministry, Brother Andre devoted his efforts to first constructing a chapel to St. Joseph, and later, the current St. Joseph's Oratory.

St. Joseph's Oratory is known for its healing oil. Since Blessed Andre used oil to heal people, visitors today still come to this church to obtain the oil. I, too, wanted some of the oil that Blessed Andre used to heal people.

As during my trip to San Diego, I had gout during this trip as well. So there I was on crutches, slowly climbing the snow-covered steps of this huge church. (I hadn't realized there would be six inches of snow in Montreal in April!) Hobbling step by step, I made my way to the church. However, by the time I finally ascended the stairs, it was too late in the day for me to get any of the oil.

The next day, I took a train to Quebec in order to visit another healing site, the Shrine of St. Anne, the grandmother of Jesus. A beautiful church, it is also a place where people are healed; as a result, thousands of crutches have been left behind.

Only after I got home from Montréal did I realize I had forgotten to go back to St. Joseph's Oratory for the oil. Fortunately, I know a lady whose daughter, a nun, was going to go on a pilgrimage to the Oratory, so I asked her to get some oil for me, and that's how I finally got it!

Some time later, I was at a baptism party for one of the lady's granddaughters. One of her brothers asked me to bless him with the oil. He didn't consider himself Catholic — years before, he had left the Catholic Church. But when I blessed him with the St. Joseph's oil, he was healed of cancer.

This man, who had not set foot in a Catholic church for years, came to a healing Mass to give his testimony. How beautiful it was that even though he had stopped practicing his Faith, the Lord still touched him through a Catholic priest. It's true that other people had been praying for him, but the Lord used the oil and my prayer to bring him to a place where he never in a million years thought he would return: the Catholic Church.

11

BURIED TREASURE

This story involves a yellow Punch Buggy. (If you don't know what a Punch Buggy is, it's a Volkswagen Beetle.)

I like to save money for when I want to buy a new car, and then I give my old car to my sister. So far I've given her three cars. The last car I gave her was a Toyota Corolla with about 25,000 miles on it — a relatively new car. Then I bought myself a new car.

One day, I was exercising at the gym in Fredericksburg, when at the gym was a man named Roger — whom I would describe as an eccentric Protestant millionaire. Roger had a yellow Punch Buggy that he wanted to sell.

I once attended an event with Roger. While we were dining at a restaurant, he gave me a check for $5,000 for a bishop's campaign. By giving me the check, Roger said he wanted to demonstrate to a "certain priest" (someone other than me!) that all the priest had to do was ask Roger for the money, and he would have given him $5,000.

Roger gave me his phone number, so I called him later and left this message: "Hey, Roger, this is Fr. Stefan. You're the one who taught me, 'Ask, and it will be given you; seek, and you will find; knock, and it will be opened to you' (Mt 7:7)." After quoting Scripture, I continued, "Roger, I just have this feeling that you are supposed to give me your yellow Bug for free. If this has any appeal at all, then here is my address."

I left this message fully expecting that Roger would give me his yellow Bug... however, Roger never called me back!

One Sunday during Mass, I told this story from the pulpit. The next thing I knew, everyone was giving me little yellow Matchbox Punch Buggies.

Later, while preparing another homily, I was reading a book about a saint, a nun who didn't have enough money to undertake all her projects. She took what little money she did have and gave it to the priest, lamenting to him that she didn't have enough money. The priest — now a saint and, regrettably, whose name I forget — took the money outside and buried it in the ground. He said to the sister, "Let us pray that this money will grow." This story stayed with me as I continued to receive a fleet of Matchbox cars from my many well-wishers.

A couple of days later, I went to Pittsburgh to visit my sister and her three children. During an outing, the kids and I were sitting in my car waiting at a red light. I took the little Matchbox Punch Buggy off my dashboard and said to them, "See this little Punch Buggy? I'm going to bury this in the ground, and it's going to grow into a big Punch Buggy. This little one is a Punch Buggy seed. It's going to grow into a full, live Bug."

As we were sitting there at the light, a yellow Bug pulled up right next to us. I motioned to the driver to put the window down. I felt comfortable doing this because there seems to be camaraderie among people who drive Bugs, although at the time I was driving a Toyota Corolla. I told the passengers of the yellow Punch Buggy that when you see someone who has a Bug and you also have a Bug, which I would in the future, they owe you a cup of coffee and a little dessert. Next, I explained to them how I was going to bury the Punch Buggy seed. I asked if they wanted a Punch Buggy seed, and I threw a yellow Matchbox car into their car. It just seemed like the right thing to do!

When I returned home, I thought about my promise to my niece and nephews to bury a Punch Buggy seed. I figured if I was going to plant a Punch Buggy seed, I needed to keep the birds and animals away, so I went to a Halloween store and bought a beautiful scarecrow. Back from the store, I planted the seed and placed the scarecrow on top of it. I showed the kids at St. Patrick's my Punch Buggy garden and told them that the seed would grow into an adult Punch Buggy.

Later, when I was driving with a friend, I said to him, "If I see a yellow Punch Buggy in the next thirty seconds, I'm going to get a Punch Buggy." We turned a corner, and sure enough, there was a yellow Punch Buggy.

The next day after a doctor's appointment, I stopped at a car dealership on my way home. Although the Toyota Corolla I was driving was only five months old and had only 8,000 miles on it, I entered the dealership and told them that I had half an hour and I wanted to trade my Corolla in for a yellow Punch Buggy. Within thirty minutes, I had my yellow Punch Buggy. I immediately drove back to St. Patrick's and parked the adult Punch Buggy next to the scarecrow. The Punch Buggy and scarecrow looked very cute side by side. When the kindergarteners and first-graders saw it, they of course thought that the Punch Buggy seed had really grown into an adult Punch Buggy.

During the time that the scarecrow was still guarding the Punch Buggy seed, I found a note on my desk that instructed me to go outside to the scarecrow. Once there, I would find something at its feet. I followed the instructions, and at the scarecrow's feet was a bag with three diamond rings in it.

Since I had buried a Punch Buggy seed, I now buried the rings and then promptly forgot about them. Within a couple of months, the gardeners had cut down all the plants near the Punch Buggy garden that would have indicated where I buried the rings.

Then one day, I was visiting the fourth-grade class at the school and told them the story about the Punch Buggy seed. At the same time, I remembered the diamonds, so I shared that story with them, too. But the next day, a mother approached me about it.

"Fr. Stefan," she said, "my son told me this tall tale about how there are diamonds buried in the field over there. I told my son that he knows how Fr. Stefan likes to tell tall tales."

"Well," I said, "I want you to go tell your son that what he told you is absolutely true. There are three diamonds buried over there."

The next day, three or four of the students who believed my story began digging in the field. Without the scarecrow and the surrounding plants as markers, it was extremely difficult to find where the rings were buried. However, once they found the first ring, they quickly also found the second and third ones. Having been successful in finding the buried treasure, the children took the booty of diamond rings home.

This event reminds me of the Scripture:

> "The kingdom of heaven is like a treasure buried in a field,
> which a person finds and hides again, and out of joy goes
> and sells all that he has and buys that field."
>
> — Mt 13:44, NAB

I remember being struck by how many other things that the children found buried in the field. They found little toy cars, toy people, money, notes, and an assortment of other objects that I hadn't buried there, but others had buried as an act of faith. When I buried the Punch Buggy seed, I told the kindergarten, first, and second grades to visit the garden to say their prayers. It was very beautiful to witness their trust and faith in God as they visited the garden. Now, every time the children see a Punch Buggy, they will remember the story of the Punch Buggy seed, and it will remind them to have faith and to trust in the Lord to let things grow.

At times, faith needs to be a little bit "ridiculous."

Some of the parents related to me cute stories about their children digging holes in the backyard and burying little toy horses and toy soldiers that they wanted to grow. In the same way the Punch Buggy seed grew, we ask the Lord to grow our own little seeds of faith that we have planted in the garden of our souls.

12

CURSES, EVIL SPIRITS, AND GENERATIONAL HEALING

In all my seminary training, we were taught very little about the devil or evil spirits. I think our professors would have said that they theoretically accepted the devil, but this teaching was not included in the seminary curriculum.

I was sleeping in my room one night when I was struck by a lightning bolt. It was a spiritual lightning bolt, not a physical one. I felt it hit my head and go into my hands, centering on my right hand. It threw me into an epileptic fit on the bed. I looked at my arm and saw that it was pulsating with what felt like a thousand volts of electricity. It was scary not to have any control over my body. So I cried, "Jesus, let it stop!" And it stopped.

The next day as I was praying, I inquired, "Jesus, what happened to me?" I took my Bible and opened it at random to Paul's letter to the Colossians, 1:12-14. The verse relates how God the Father has given us forgiveness of sin and the redemption of our bodies. He has brought us out of the kingdom of darkness and into the kingdom of light. He has brought us to the inheritance of the saints in light. What a perfect verse! It was then that I knew Jesus was taking me out of the kingdom of darkness and bringing me into the kingdom of light.

I called a good friend who was an exorcist — he knew more about this kind of thing than anyone else I'd ever met — and asked him what had happened to me. He said the Lord had given me a sovereign deliverance from the power of evil. My initial thought was, *Satan, now that you have revealed yourself, I am going to fight you until I'm free.*

Later that day, I looked at my face in a mirror. I could clearly see that there was something evil inside of me that I was battling. I saw an image of my face being contorted, and I could hear ugly noises coming out of me. Instead of being scared, however, I thought, *If this is something not of God, I will fight it to the absolute end.* I prayed in tongues and there were all sorts of reactions. My face became hard and would make expressions that seemed unnatural; tongues became ugly and guttural, and I knew this was not of God, so I was determined to pray until I was free.

I never thought in a million years that there would be something evil in me or around me. My whole life I had been dealing with a depression that I was never able to conquer. It made sense to me then that perhaps at least some of the depression was due to evil.

Frankly, I think there's actually more evil around us than we know. The devil doesn't want himself to be known because once he's known, his gig is up. When the devil isn't threatened by how we live, he prefers to remain hidden. It is said that Satan's greatest victory is convincing us that he does not exist.

However, the Baptism in the Holy Spirit penetrates us so deeply that it draws or forces evil out. When we pray in tongues, in the Spirit, we are praying from such a deep part of us that the devil has no place to hide. Thus, he must reveal himself. When he does reveal himself, it is a sign that he is about to leave.

The devil is all smoke and mirrors. I liken him to the wizard in the Wizard of Oz. Remember how the wizard was all smoke and mirrors? For the most part, so is the devil.

Previously, I had experienced another encounter with the devil when I was in my second year of the seminary and working at a parish. I was driving down the street when I heard a voice say, "Drive off the road. There is nothing for you." I thought to myself, *I just heard the devil.* I wondered to myself why the devil would be interested in me. I also thought, *What a perfect description of the devil — nothingness.* God is the fullness of being, and the devil is nothingness.

Following the deliverance from the power of evil, I continued to pray throughout other evil manifestations. On the feast day of Our Lady of Lourdes, I went to a healing service; during Mass, when the Eucharist was elevated by the priest, I fell into a fetal position and started uttering malicious tongues.

This was the first time I ever reacted to an evil presence while around other people; every other time I had been alone. I believe it was necessary for this evil to be manifested so that this priest would be able to help me. I received prayers from him and others that night, and over the course of the next five years. I can truly say it was a battle against evil.

I remember meeting a young lady named Claudia who attended the prayer meetings. At one meeting I noticed that when I would look at her, I could see a key around her neck — not a physical key, but one I "saw" in the Spirit — and had this sense that whomever she prayed for would be healed. I approached her and told her this. I also asked her if she would pray for me, and she agreed to.

When she prayed over me, I saw a vision of a soldier on a winged horse who, I believe, was St. George. St. George was a soldier who fought the devil, and so I believed it was St. George who appeared to me because I know that I'm called to be a soldier for Christ, and part of my vocation is to fight the devil. The man in the vision handed me a sword with my name on the crossguard. He said to me, "You are the holder of the sword."

As this young lady finished praying for me, I came out of the vision. Before I said a thing to her, she told me "Fr. Stefan, I want to tell you what I saw when I prayed over you. I saw a flaming sword, and Mary was praying behind the sword." In essence, she saw what I saw.

The Book of Revelation says that we will be given a white stone with a new name — a name given to us by the Lord (see Rev 2:17). It is not a proper name, but a descriptive name. In the Bible, a name change indicates a new mission. God changes Abram's name to Abraham (see Gen 17:5), and Jesus changes Simon's name to Peter. Peter is "the Rock of the Church" (see Mt 16:18). The white stone with the new name is our deepest vocation.

Exactly one year and one day after being hit by the bolt of lightning, I was at a Pentecostal church for a prayer meeting. As I was there praising the Lord, I was struck again by another bolt of lightning — only this time, the voltage was about 10,000 times stronger! My whole body was pulsating with electricity. It was like I was holding on to an electric fence — like I was Electric Man in a comic book. I fell to the ground, and my friend Fr. Paul came over and touched my shoulder. The electricity went through him, too. It seemed like enough electricity to kill a person and lasted about two minutes. But when I got up, I was not injured in any way. I was fine. I wondered why this had happened to me again exactly one year later.

I soon learned why. Around the same time I was hit by lightning the second time, I found out that my father's cousin had just had a family tree completed by a professional. When I looked at the family tree, the researcher for our family history reported that there was nothing remarkable about our family tree... except one thing

My great-great-grandfather had seven children. Two of his sons, Andrew and Stefan Starzynski (my namesake), lived in Pittsburgh, Pennsylvania, and owned a hotel/hostel/bar on Carson Street that still exists today. Our family history shows that Andrew and Stefan were murdered by a Fr. Ludwig, a defrocked Polish Catholic priest, in 1907. The interesting fact is that the murders of my great-uncles happened on the same day and at the same hour that I was struck twice by lightning.

My family has the newspaper clippings from the day of the murders. It appears that after Andrew and Stefan Starzynski threw

Fr. Ludwig out of the bar or hotel, for reasons unknown, Fr. Ludwig came back later and murdered them. He was found guilty of premeditated murder and spent many years in prison. The article concluded with the amazing fact that 30,000 people attended the funerals of Andrew and Stefan Starzynski.

(Interestingly enough, my sister currently lives in Pittsburgh. She cleans houses to earn extra money, and she has cleaned the house where the murders took place.)

After the murders, I'm sure that many of my ancestors would have uttered curses against priests. But I don't think it is an accident that my namesake, Stefan, was murdered by a priest — and ninety years later, I became a Catholic priest, and those curses uttered throughout the years fell on me. The lightning bolts that struck me were connected to the murders in my family.

In the same way that physical conditions such as alcoholism, depression, or heart disease run in families, spiritual conditions can run through families as well. When it comes to physical maladies, a doctor asks his patients questions about the family medical history. However, sometimes illnesses are rooted in generational attitudes or sins. For example, sometimes events like abortion, unexpected deaths, or infant deaths run in families. I believe this is true, in large part, because of personal experience. I have prayed with people who appear to be suffering from incurable conditions, but when I've prayed for healing of the generations, I've seen remarkable results.

In a way, generational healing is similar to what we believe about baptism. Baptism heals the effects of original sin. Even though babies have done nothing wrong, the sin of Adam and Eve is still passed on to them. Just as baptism heals the effect of original sin, generational healing takes care of the effects of generational sin.

I used to visit a lady named Mary at the hospital. She had about ten different illnesses, any one of which could have killed her. Over the course of a year, I saw an odd pattern take place: each time I'd go to visit her, the doctors would give her only a month to live; she'd then bounce back, only to be in the hospital a few months later.

One day, she asked me if I believed that a curse could cause an illness. I told her I did believe that and asked her to tell me her story.

"When I sleep at night," she said, "I hear a man's voice speaking through my mouth." I asked her where she thought it came from, and she related how she used to see an occultist for over fifteen years — much of her adult life. The occultist would make all her decisions for her; she would never do anything without first consulting this woman, who would use Tarot cards and other devices of the occult. Mary told me that when she broke off her relationship with this person, the lady told her that in one year's time she would be deathly ill. That was exactly what happened.

I remembered an instance when Fr. McAlear told me when he went to visit someone in a hospital in serious condition, he had the sense to "break the curse." He told me that when he broke the curse, the person's back arched in the air and then came down — and the person was subsequently healed.

Mary also related that she could never enter a Catholic Church. If she did, she would throw up. She also couldn't physically be around anything holy, such as medals or holy cards.

Finally, during one of my hospital visits, I told her that I wanted to go to her house and pray with her. Once she was well enough to go home, although she was confined to bed, I went to her house. I took all the things the occultist had given her like amulets, books, and other things, and said a prayer over them, covering them in the Precious Blood of Jesus. I disposed of everything by throwing it all in the sewer, then went back into her house to pray with her. As we began, I prayed in English, but nothing seemed to happen. Then I started praying in tongues.

St. Paul tells us about a variety of tongues. There are praise tongues, tongues of deliverance, tongues of healing, and even tongues to help create joy and laughter. Each type of tongue serves a different purpose. A variety of tongues can also mean that each person has their own prayer language, and over time they might have even more than one prayer language. The Holy Spirit gives the person what is needed at any given time and situation. One of the reasons I pray in tongues at the healing Masses is because the Holy Spirit knows what the person needs in terms of healing. When there is an evil spirit involved, the Holy Spirit seems to give the person praying the right words or tongues to address and deal with the evil spirit.

Mary had never had a charismatic experience in her life. As I was praying over her in tongues, she said, "Fr. Stefan, this *something* is telling you to stop."

I responded with, "If something is telling me to stop, we must be on the right track." I continued to pray over her, and she started to describe this hideous face with red eyes that she was seeing. She said it was telling me to stop.

We had only been praying for about ten minutes when I saw Jesus appear in the room. He was wearing a white robe. I said to myself, *If Jesus is here, we're in good shape.*

Without me mentioning anything to her, Mary then spoke up. "I see Jesus as a high priest in white robes," she said, and I realized we were both seeing the same thing. She went on to describe how she saw one large serpent and five small serpents, and Jesus wiped them away with a motion of his hand.

The next day, Mary was out of bed and doing fine after having been deathly ill for a year. Her one desire was to be a chef, and she was able to go back to being a chef after this deliverance.

This experience was truly shocking to me. Casting out evil spirits and people receiving healing happened in the Bible. It seemed like I was living in biblical times rather than the reality of the present day.

Mary's mother didn't know that I had been at their house praying with Mary before she was healed. Shortly thereafter, Mary's mother beckoned me to come to their house to pray. She said that whenever she tried to sleep, she looked up and saw a demon above her bed — and I realized that the demon her mother was seeing was the same demon that had been knocked out of Mary.

———————

The parents of a young girl had asked me to pray for her. Jill was in the seventh grade and having lots of troubles. When I prayed for her, it almost appeared as if there was a demonic spirit against her. She screamed and hollered as I tried to pray with her. I was not afraid; rather, I felt encouraged as I prayed with her.

I thought that we should do a generational healing Mass, that maybe Jill's problem was rooted in the past. So I went to her house and celebrated a generational healing Mass with both Jill's parents, along with Jill's mother's sister and one other person. We trusted that the Holy Spirit would give us an image or word as we went back fifteen generations. After Communion, I waited for the Holy Spirit to reveal something, but nothing became apparent to us that evening.

The next evening, I was in my room at St. Patrick's when, at about midnight, my door opened and a presence entered my room. Just then, the phone rang. The pastor answered it and called for me to pick up the call. It was Jill's mother.

"Fr. Stefan," she said, "I need a word of the Holy Spirit from you right now. My father just had a heart attack, and it looks like he might die."

This occurrence was weird because her father hadn't even been sick . . . until this day. Jill's mother didn't know that her father was already dead, but I knew he was the person who had entered my room.

During the Mass the previous evening, we had asked for forgiveness for the past. Jill's grandfather was a deeply troubled man who didn't have much religion or faith. He actually kept a gun near his bed, and the family was always worried about him.

In a moment of panic, I thought, *Oh my gosh! Did my prayer kill this man?* But as I listened to the family's reflection, they said that if there was ever a time for him to die, it was now — the day after a Mass had been offered and the day after we had asked for forgiveness. I truly believe that Jill's grandfather went to heaven. Interestingly enough, Jill got better. It's almost as if her grandfather took the curse to the grave, and therefore, she was healed.

One day, a boy named Chris came to my office. He said he could hear the voices of demons and witches speaking to him. He could also see images of castles. When he mentioned castles, I immediately thought of England. I asked him and his mother if their family had any association with England. The mother told me that they had lived in England, and it was where Chris was born.

Immediately I decided to do a healing Mass for the generations. Again, we went back fifteen generations on both of his parents' sides and asked the Holy Spirit to reveal anything that might need healing. When you go back fifteen generations, it's amazing what you will find. Among other things, the Holy Spirit revealed events such as murder, rape, abortion, drowning, and people killed by fire.

After we did the Mass, Chris no longer heard the voices or saw horrid images. Before this, he could not attend Mass. It seemed as if he was prevented from going. Now, he can go to Mass, although still with a bit of difficulty. Sometimes, even though an evil presence has been cast out of a person, there is still demonic residue remaining in the person that continues to affect them. Sometimes, our thinking also needs to be changed. We are so in the habit of being afraid that we still act out of fear — not knowing that we have been set free.

13

THE CIRCLE IS COMPLETE

It has given me great joy to write this book. I have loved looking back and reflecting on all the beautiful ways God has worked in my life and in the lives of others. However, as I write this final part, I now write with a heart filled with sadness. My good friend, Monica Zimmer, has just died. She was only forty-five years old. She was getting ready to go out with friends when she had a seizure, hit her head, and died. Her death reminds me that all life is fragile and that we are called to love one another in every moment.

Monica was the daughter of Frank and Hildegard. Right now, I am looking out upon the ocean from their home, set right on the shore. It was this house that I came to, two weeks before my ordination, and read a book on the Holy Spirit that changed my life and influenced how I live my vocation.

The past few days, I have been helping Frank and Hilde with the funeral arrangements, as we wait for family and friends to arrive for the funeral. One of Monica's friends that we're waiting for is Mary Beth Page (see Chapter 1 about how Mary Beth asked me to pray for A.J. on my ordination day).

As much as we don't understand fully why God heals some and not others, we also don't understand why someone as young as Monica is no longer with us. We read in the Bible:

For who has known the mind of the Lord, or who has been his counselor?

— Rom 11:34

"For as the heavens are higher than the earth, so are my ways higher your ways and my thoughts than your thoughts."

. — Is 55:9

In his encyclical *God is Love*, Pope Benedict reminds us that St. Augustine says the same thing in different words: "If you can understand him, it is not God."

Monica's death reminds me of the words I spoke at Jacob's funeral (see Chapter 8). I reflected on how I had given him the relic of Blessed Faustina and how the relic returned to me at his death. I had said at his funeral that everything seems to come full circle — or, as it is sometimes said, we end where we have often begun. Right now, I am sitting at the house where many of the stories from this book began, and everything does seem to have come full circle.

In this book, I have told you about many great stories like the Paul Stefan Home. We have opened two homes so far. We hope that in five years, we will have many more homes — dozens of them — and, as years go by, to have hundreds, if not thousands. I have learned that God can do anything with those who have faith. Mother Teresa said it this way:

> God will use you to accomplish great things on the condition that you believe in His love much more than in your own weakness.

I have told you about many healings. I trust that Jesus will work many more healings. I trust that, in God's timing, I will stand before hundreds of thousands of people proclaiming the love and healing power of Jesus. I expect to see many, many more people receive the healing touch of Jesus. I am also continuing to learn that God has his timing, and that his timing is perfect. I hope and pray that when I die I can say, "The circle is complete."

For now, this circle is complete. God bless you all; you are in my prayers.

TESTIMONIES

PAUL'S STORY

by Evelyn James

In April of 2005, my husband, Randy, and I received the wonderful news that we were expecting our sixth baby. I knew in my heart that this was Paul. Years before, it came to me during prayer that we had not yet had Paul. Through additional signs, we had a sense that Paul was going to be a very special child of God.

I must admit, though, that we were concerned when we learned of the pregnancy. During my previous pregnancy with Rebekah, our fifth child, I had been diagnosed with gestational diabetes; I had to inject myself daily with insulin. Now, unfortunately, my doctor informed me that this condition was unavoidable.

Randy and I had been told by many parishioners at our church that our priest, Fr. Stefan, had the gift of healing. I immediately contacted Fr. Stefan early in my pregnancy, and he prayed over me. As a result of his prayers, not only did I avoid the daily insulin shots, but throughout the entire pregnancy, the results of every glucose test fell well within the normal range. There is no doubt that a healing took place.

I had my first sonogram on September 15, the feast of Our Lady of Sorrows. Viewing the sonogram, the technician detected a problem and alerted the doctor. After studying the sonogram himself, the doctor informed me that our baby had a diaphragmatic hernia, a hole in the diaphragm. This hernia would allow the abdominal organs to be pulled into the chest cavity and thereby prevent normal lung development. The physician gave me this one-minute definition and then asked if I would like to consider terminating my pregnancy. I was crying as I tried to comprehend the horrific words coming from the doctor's mouth. I had just viewed our beautiful baby; I had watched it moving and growing inside me. Again we called on Fr. Stefan for prayers and a miracle.

In October, we invited Fr. Stefan to our home for dinner. Prior to his arrival, I had an overwhelming curiosity to look at September 15 on a *Chicken Soup for the Christian Soul* calendar, a compilation of inspirational messages from all the *Chicken Soup* books. I had not kept up with this calendar, so the top page was an inspirational message from one day in June. I flipped the pages to the 15th of September, the date we were told of our baby's condition, and found an entry "A Mother's Journey," that spoke of "A precious little baby with... *an amazing set of lungs.*"

Knowing our baby didn't have lungs, we considered this a message to keep believing and praying for our baby's health. I did notice, in flipping through the pages of the calendar, that this was the only inspirational message that came from *Chicken Soup for the Expectant Mother's Soul*; to me, this was another sign, and I couldn't wait to show Father when he arrived that evening. We took his advice to put the September 15 reflection on our refrigerator and to read it daily. Fr. Stefan told us to expect a miracle!

Later in October, we received a call from a friend letting us know that Fr. Stefan was on a trip to Mexico. She told us of his plans to visit the Shrine of Our Lady of Guadalupe and to include our baby's condition in his prayers. Around this same time, we learned from the recent sonogram that our baby was a boy. We immediately named him Paul. We also had decided on his middle name, but we wanted to keep that as a surprise.

Fr. Stefan encouraged us to attend his healing Masses, held one Saturday a month. During one healing Mass in November, Fr. Stefan quoted Mother Angelica: "If you are willing to do the ridiculous, God will do the miraculous." He asked all of us to make an act of faith. At this point in my pregnancy, we were advised by several doctors to travel to Kansas to secure a legal late-term abortion. Paul's condition was worsening: his intestines, stomach, and kidneys were in the chest cavity — not only pushing his heart to one side but preventing little, if any, lung tissue to develop. In response to Fr. Stefan's request for an act of faith, and desperately wanting a miracle of healing for Paul, we made a bold proclamation to personally take part in the pro-life movement. We had decided that, whether Paul lived or went to be with our Lord in heaven, we would volunteer in a pro-life organization. We discussed Project Rachel, a mission related to the healing of women after abortion, as an option.

So many lovely people from our parish had also been praying for Paul. We prayed constantly — saying the rosary, the Divine Mercy Chaplet, various novenas, and attending Mass as frequently as possible. Fr. Stefan met us on many occasions to pray. After praying, he would open his Bible at random and read the Scripture. Each and every time, the verse he opened to had great meaning and encouraged us to continue praying for Paul's healing. During our last visit with Fr. Stefan, he read a passage from the Bible about a baby being born alive. This was contrary to all the doctors, who said Paul would die before birth. Fr. Stefan boldly told us that day that Paul would be born alive!

On the morning of December 12, the feast of Our Lady of Guadalupe, I awoke with more pain than usual. At this point, due to Paul's condition, the quantity of amniotic fluid was well over the normal amount. I had refused the technique of inserting a needle into the amniotic sac to withdraw some of the excess fluid. We did not want to increase the chances of an early labor. Paul was not due for another five weeks, so I refused to think I was in labor.

But although I wanted to attend Mass, I couldn't seem to manage the pain, as it increased throughout the morning and afternoon. Randy picked up our children from school that day. That very day, a parishioner I had met only once had given our daughter, Rachel, a framed picture of Our Lady of Guadalupe. This picture had been brought back from Mexico by Fr. Stefan at the request of this woman. On it she had placed a sticky note that said to place our hands on Our Lady's picture while praying. We did this together, and by 11:00 p.m., I called my doctor to say that I was leaving for the hospital.

We took the image of Our Lady of Guadalupe with us to the hospital and were greeted by a Catholic nurse who happened to be my dear friend's sister and knew Paul's story. She told us how that very morning when she arrived at work, she reached for something in her glove compartment and a rosary had dropped into her hand. Although she did not typically carry a rosary with her, she put it in her uniform pocket. As she handed it to me to use, we all noticed that the rosary included the image of Our Lady of Guadalupe. Randy and I told her that we had never seen one like this before; we knew that Our Lady was making herself known to us.

After a brief exam, not only was it confirmed that I was in labor, but my cervix was dilated nine centimeters. An emergency C-section was unavoidable. But the pain I experienced during this labor was not nearly as severe as the pain I had experienced during labor with our other children. All of our prayers were being heard!

While the surgery was being performed, the doctors, nurses, and Randy were concentrating on Paul's delivery, not knowing exactly what to expect. Paul was immediately whisked away to a prepared area in the room and an intubation procedure was attempted in order to inflate any lung tissue that might have developed.

One of the nurses stood behind me during the C-section and whispered Psalm 23 and other Scriptures in my ear. Over a year later, I learned that this nurse was not seen or heard by anyone else in the room. I am convinced that my guardian angel visited me, coming to my aid in my most desperate time of need!

On December 13, at 3:00 a.m., Tammy — a perinatal bereavement nurse, whom we had met once in the doctor's office — arrived at the hospital. She brought along holy water, a camera, and a beautiful baby blanket that she had personally made for Paul. Without Tammy and Fr. Stefan, I am not sure where my husband and I would have found the strength to endure during this most critical time in our lives.

Our beautiful Paul was baptized and photographed by Tammy and died after only forty-one minutes of life. We held him and loved him and brought our other five children to the hospital to share in the memory of their baby brother that came to us for such a brief time, but will touch all of us forever.

When Fr. Stefan arrived at the hospital that day, we thanked him for his unceasing prayers and, in honor of him, we named our precious baby Paul Stefan. (Father's name is Stefan Paul Starzynski.)

On December 17, Fr. Stefan celebrated the funeral Mass for Paul Stefan. He was laid to rest in Baby Land at a cemetery close to our home. Knowing that I was still in recovery from the surgery, a friend of Fr. Stefan's brought a meal to our home after the funeral. She mentioned to Randy that she had been praying a novena to St. Andrew with Fr. Stefan, in regards to establishing a home for unwed mothers.

After she left, Randy and I discussed this and became convinced that God was calling us to help establish this home. Randy and I agreed to find out more about the novena to St. Andrew that Fr. Stefan and his friend had been praying.

Five weeks later — on the very morning we had said to each other that it was time to call Father's friend — Randy ran into her in the parking lot of a grocery store. The following morning, she and six other people gathered at our home for what was to become the beginning of the Paul Stefan Home Foundation. We discussed many topics that morning, but the primary focus was on how to raise the funds necessary to build a home.

Fr. Stefan, on a trip to Israel, continued his prayers and offered his Masses for the establishment of a home for single expectant mothers. The Saturday night he returned home, he celebrated a healing Mass. In an act of faith, five people gave him $1,000 each for that intention. The following day, after the Sunday morning Mass, a parishioner told Father about two beautiful vacant farmhouses nearby, on seventy acres of land owned by a pipeline company. After discussions with the company, an agreement was made for the company to lease the two farmhouses to the Paul Stefan Foundation for one dollar a year.

While waiting for the approval from the company, Fr. Stefan invited several of us to attend a Mass celebrated at one of the homes. During his homily that day, as he prayed for the end to abortion, he stated the need for these homes nationwide. He told us that the pipeline company had built these homes for their employees; they extended from the Southwest all the way to New Jersey. He also prayed to acquire additional homes to help women in other areas of our country.

At that very moment, the Holy Spirit revealed to me the meaning of the September 15th inspirational message from the *Chicken Soup* Calendar. Paul's "lungs" *are* amazing — not earthly lungs, but heavenly lungs created to breathe into existence homes for expectant mothers, to provide them an alternative to abortion in a loving, caring environment. It all makes so much sense to us now! There is no doubt that we were called to join Fr. Stefan in his mission.

In the following weeks, the necessary planning began to take place. A board of directors was formed, the application for a special use permit was submitted, renovations were made to the homes, and the decision to call these safe havens "The Paul Stefan Home of Our Lady of Guadalupe" was made public knowledge. On September 10, 2006, we held our first Paul Stefan Home Open House with approximately 250 guests attending. Fr. Stefan spoke that day and brought it to our attention that it was almost exactly nine months from December 13 — Paul Stefan's birth and death — to September 10, the birth of the first Paul Stefan Home.

The first call for accommodations at the Paul Stefan Home came from a nearby homeless shelter. After the initial interview, Erin became our first resident. Erin had received very little prenatal care, so we immediately made an appointment for her with the Health Department. The doctor told her she was having a boy, due between December 2 and 26. Erin decided to name her baby

Andrew. Erin knew nothing about the St. Andrew Novena that Fr. Stefan and his friend had prayed the previous year. St. Andrew was the "conception" that had brought about the Paul Stefan Homes.

On December 12, 2006, the feast of Our Lady of Guadalupe, Erin went into labor and was taken to the hospital in the next town. Andrew Nicholas was born the following day, exactly one year to the day that our Paul Stefan was born and died. We know that Our Lady and Lord have given us this beautiful gift of Andrew as a confirmation to continue our mission to house women and babies in need.

Fr. Stefan Starzynski's devotion and faith have influenced how we live our lives today. After two years since opening the doors to the Paul Stefan Homes, thirty women and babies have been given the opportunity to improve their lives. We combine our prayers with Fr. Stefan's that we will see the end to abortion and we continue to lovingly support women by seeking other homes in all areas around the country.

FR. BAKER'S INTERCESSION

by Deborah L. Hennessy

I began my battle with melanoma cancer almost three years ago. Most people tend to think that melanoma is "just skin cancer," but this isn't true. Melanoma is the second most aggressive tumor type, right behind pancreatic cancer. Sixty thousand Americans will be diagnosed this year, and eight thousand will die. In the United States, one person dies of melanoma each hour of every day. Sadly, it is the number-one killer of woman ages 25 to 35.

Melanoma does not respond to traditional chemotherapy or radiation therapy, as other cancers do. The only FDA-approved treatment for Stage 4 MM (metastatic melanoma) is Interleukin, or IL-2, which was developed thirty years ago. Since then, no great strides have been made in the treatment of melanoma. Only 26 percent of the people treated with IL-2 will experience a "partial response," i.e., some shrinkage or no new growth (stable) of tumors. Only 7 percent will experience a complete response. Of these 7 percent, remission will last anywhere from four months to ten years, the average remission being 4.9 years.

In February 2006, I had the skin and some muscle removed from my right shoulder and a flap of skin from my back moved up to cover the large defect. I then had twenty-five radiation treatments. Within eight months, PET/CT scans showed the melanoma had progressed to Stage 4, invading both my lungs. I had part of my right lung removed. My medical oncologist at Johns Hopkins told me I had a life expectancy of six to nine months. Generally, Stage 4 does not exceed twelve months. There is no Stage 5.

This oncologist was not aggressive and exhibited a defeatist attitude, so I knew I had to find my own path to wellness. I got busy educating myself and decided upon IL-2 treatments. I was admitted to Henrico Doctors Hospital in Richmond, VA, for this regimen. I was infused every eight hours with IL-2 and was able to tolerate ten treatments per week, although I was very sick. To say IL-2 is toxic is an understatement. I have very little recollection of my treatment weeks; that is a blessing in itself. My husband or a dear friend watched over me, along with intensive-care providers.

After my fourth week of IL-2, my oncologist determined it was too toxic for me to continue treatment. I challenged him: "Melanoma is terminal, so what is more toxic — treatment, or sure death from the disease?" After pleading with him on two different visits, I sought out another oncologist.

Luckily, I found another melanoma specialist and he agreed to finish the IL-2 protocol, another two weeks of treatment. Each of the six weeks brought a twenty- to thirty-pound weight gain; burned, blistered, itchy skin; nausea, vomiting, and diarrhea; insomnia; hallucinations; renal failure; thrombocytopenia (drop in blood platelets needed for clotting); and rigors (violent shivering) after each dose. The IL-2 treatments cause bone marrow depression, hence the thrombocytopenia, which can result in fatal bleeding or hemorrhage.

My first week of treatment was halted due to my platelets falling to 150,000 to 40,000. The bone marrow depression was an issue for each week of my six weeks of treatment. Recovery from the other side effects took an additional week.

I had PET/CT scans every three months. I was told my February 27, 2008, scans were clear, but I remained cautious. My May 28, 2008, PET/CT scans showed a 3-mm nodule/lesion in my right lung field — not where I had the lung resection. I returned to Richmond for a dedicated CT of my chest and an MRI of my brain. Three days later, without results, I left on a flight to Buffalo, NY.

On June 6, my return flight from Buffalo was late. I found an empty seat and waited. After a few minutes, the gentleman next to me started to chat. I hadn't noticed his collar at first, but when he introduced himself as Fr. Stefan Starzynski, I told him I was a member of a Catholic church in Virginia.

Fr. Stefan told me of his pilgrimage to the shrine of Fr. Nelson Baker and of his good works. He told me of the "visitation" of a man he did not know to his room one night. Later, he would come to find this was Fr. Baker. Although this was an unusual story, I didn't find it impossible to believe; I know God does work in mysterious ways. My faith and beliefs have brought me this far, and I had no doubt of Fr. Stefan's encounter. As I look back, I realize that was the first step in what was to happen — my mind and heart were open.

I told Fr. Stefan about my battle with cancer. I was not defeated or depressed. In fact, I have come to know many blessings because of cancer. I told him my faith had carried me through the hardest of times, and I was not afraid. As a registered nurse, I'm very open and candid about my situation. I find in talking to others, I can help in navigating the health care system, calm anxieties, or give hope when all hope seems lost. That may very well be God's plan for me. I have no answer as to why I am still here when others, so many others, have passed. I have known all my life that God has a plan for me.

Our very late plane arrived at last. Just as they called us for boarding, Fr. Stefan asked if he could lay hands on me and pray for a healing, and I said yes. We stood, and he placed both hands on my head and prayed for my healing, petitioning Fr. Baker to intercede on my behalf.

As Fr. Stefan prayed aloud, in Gate 4, Buffalo Airport, I felt a calmness and peace wash over me. It was as if everything stood still. I know there must have been many eyes on us, many people wondering what was happening. I wonder if they knew they were witnessing a miracle.

After Fr. Stefan prayed, he told me I was healed of cancer — cured. Then, he opened a large bag and took out a framed 11-x-14-inch picture of Fr. Baker and offered it to me. I declined because I knew he spent a bit of money on it, and I suspected it was intended for someone else, but Fr. Stefan assured me it was meant for me. Suddenly, I, too, sensed it was. He also gave me a prayer card with a piece of Fr. Baker's vestments attached.

On August 27, 2008, I had repeat PET/CT scan and a dedicated chest CT. Two days later, my oncologist called me to tell me the lesion/nodule seen in the February/May scans was gone. I then sent a thank-you note to Fr. Stefan, telling him of my healing.

On December 8, 2008, I was examined again. I requested copies of my past scans for Fr. Stefan to give to Bishop Loverde. Upon reading these scans, I found I had two additional smaller lesions in my right upper lung field. I requested to be rescanned. I talked to Fr. Stefan later that night and told him of the additional two nodules that I was unaware of. I was disappointed for Fr. Baker and myself. But then, Fr. Stefan asked me, "Debbie, do you believe you were healed?"

I said, "Yes."

December 11, 2008, the CT scan of my chest and abdomen showed no acute abnormality. An MRI of my brain was also clear. Copies of scans and doctors' progress records were given to Fr. Stefan to take to Bishop Loverde.

In 1987, Fr. Baker was elevated to Servant of God. Since then, many people have prayed for the occurrence of another miracle in hopes of his canonization.

OUR MIRACLE

by Tom and Sue Sherman

My wife, Susan, was expecting our fourth child. We were both over forty years old, and Susan had experienced a placental abruption (the separation of the placenta as it breaks away from the wall of the uterus too early) with our first child. Our firstborn, now age seventeen, had been born two and a half months premature, weighing two pounds, fourteen ounces, and had cerebral palsy. Our second and third children (ages eight and six) were both healthy and had been born without any complications.

We hadn't told anyone, with the exception of my employer, that Susan was pregnant. We were waiting until she completed the second semester (at the Catholic preschool where she worked) before our announcement. My wife was taking prenatal vitamins and was experiencing a normal pregnancy, expecting birth in mid-January.

The night of October 4, 2004, my wife felt some discomfort and had light bleeding, or spotting. But the next morning, she awoke to a pool of blood in the bed. We called 911, sent our other two children off to school, arrived at the hospital about ten minutes later, and were taken to the OB-GYN area. The doctors informed us that my wife had experienced a placental abruption again, and the baby would probably be delivered shortly.

For her previous six weeks at work, my wife had enjoyed many good conversations with Fr. Stefan, so she'd asked me to call him if anything bad happened. I immediately called him to see if he could come to the hospital, then called my employer at the Catholic academy.

Fr. Stefan was off that day but heard my message and arrived at the hospital within minutes. A few minutes later, my wife was taken to delivery to have the baby. I prayed fervently for the next few minutes, clutching the Miraculous Medal that my wife had worn and that now linked us together. The nurse came out and told us that my wife had delivered a child. When we asked what the sex was, we were told that they hadn't checked. We were also told that my wife was being attended to because she had lost a lot of blood.

The next few minutes seemed like forever. We prayed and prayed as thoughts of losing my wife and child raced through my mind. Having had my own mother die when I was three, I couldn't help thinking about our other three children and the idea of them also being raised without their mother.

At that time, the surgeon who delivered the baby came out to speak to us. He told us that Susan had lost an enormous amount of blood and that he had needed to close her quickly and in doing so may have nicked the femoral artery and/or the urethra. He said if she recovered, she might need a colostomy bag for the remainder of her life. He also told us the baby, a boy, was born dead and needed to be resuscitated. He was tiny and frail, only weighing one pound, fourteen ounces, and that the survival rate at this weight and at twenty-five and a half weeks' gestation was not very high.

After the surgeon left, they brought my wife into the recovery room. The room was directly in front of us, with two walls of windows that we could look through. Because of loss of blood and complications of her situation, her body temperature had dropped significantly. I did not know this, so when the nurse placed a warming blanket over Susan's body, including her head, I panicked — until the nurse quickly explained the reality of the situation! She had pulled the curtains so no one could see in the room anymore; all I could think about was how, not more than eight feet and a wall of windows away, my wife was in critical medical need.

I asked Fr. Stefan to perform the last rites on both my newborn son and Susan, but he refused. Instead, he told me, he would administer the sacrament of the Anointing of the Sick to Susan and the sacrament of Baptism to our son. I stood by Susan's bedside as Fr. Stefan prayed and anointed her with holy oil. Then, he told me that she was going to be fine.

Next, we started for the Neonatal Intensive Care Unit (NICU) in order to baptize my son. The nurses informed us that we would need to wait about twenty minutes while they worked on the baby, but after about five minutes, Fr. Stefan replied that we were going to baptize the baby *now*.

As we walked in the NICU, Fr. Stefan asked the nurse to bring him some water. Then he asked me the baby's name. But Susan and I had not gotten around to discussing names, nor even spoken of possible names, so I hesitated. When I told Fr. Stefan that the baby's name was James David, he asked me how I came up with the name. I told him that it was not my thought, nor was it a family name or the name of anyone I knew. Perhaps the name was given to me from James' guardian angel.

Fr. Stefan put on gloves, reached inside the incubator, and baptized my little boy, who in his brief ten minutes had now been resuscitated and baptized. Upon removing his hands from the incubator, Fr. Stefan informed me that James was going to be fine, even healthy. Father said he could feel a tremendous power coming from James when he baptized him and that he knew that the Holy Spirit was present, was accepting James and vowing to look over him.

The next hours and days were long and draining. Susan needed to have most of her blood supply replaced, and James was on a ventilator struggling to maintain his own life. Susan came home after five days, only to be readmitted two days later when she began to bleed uncontrollably from her abdomen.

James stayed at the hospital for eleven days. His guest list was limited to his parents, grandparents, and Fr. Stefan. Many family friends that were doctors also snuck in to see him and monitor his progress. After about eight days, two large growths appeared — one on the left side of James' head and the other on his right shin. They were hemangiomas, blood vessels that had not formed properly. We were told not to worry, as they should disappear over time.

I was back teaching at the Academy, where the smiles and cheers of my 500 students brought some relief and hope to me. Above the entrance to the gym where I teach is a round relief that depicts Jesus surrounded by eight children of all genders, races, and colors. He is holding a small brown-haired boy close, with Jesus' cheek pressed against the left side of the boy's head. I took considerable comfort in looking at this relief during prayer, knowing that the little brown-headed boy was James, and that Jesus was holding him close and taking care of him.

I also knew that the schoolchildren and parishioners were keeping James in their prayers. The kids served as my sounding board. I let them know of James' size, and I talked to them about the amazing power of prayer. I asked them to please continue to pray for James. However, most importantly, the children showed me the continual power of God's love.

After eleven days, we were told that James had a problem called NEC (necrotizing enterocolitis) which could severely harm the body's ability to digest food. If untreated, the condition might mean James would need a feeding tube. He also might require surgery, but there was not a pediatric NICU surgeon at the hospital where he was; he would need to be transferred to MCV Hospital, about an hour away. Our oldest child had been born at MCV and had spent eight weeks in their NICU, so we were not strangers to the trip or to the hospital.

The days and weeks went by slowly. Fortunately, the NEC resolved itself without requiring surgery or creating any problems. However, there was a major development that concerned everyone. James had been diagnosed with a Grade II bilateral brain bleed, meaning both sides of his brain had small leaks of blood. Grade II was on a scale of I-IV. We were told that it might heal itself, or it might progress to a worsened state.

During one visit, we witnessed the medical students make their rounds and present their findings to the doctors. As we sat next to James, who just seemed like a tiny toy baby with tubes and wires protruding from everywhere, we heard the students mention a Grade IV bilateral brain bleed. After looking at the notes, I saw where it was written as a Grade III and a Grade IV. Grade IV carries a 90 percent chance of fatality.

Once again, we were facing a major obstacle, and our one-hour ride home seemed like twenty hours. This latest development tested our imagination and faith. Our son was fighting, as were we, but we needed more prayers and more strength.

One month after James was born, Fr. Stefan accompanied us to MCV to see James. As we sat by James, we were aware of the two babies adjacent to James that had similar birth weights and gestation times. The one to his left would die the following week while we sat with James, providing us with another reminder of how tenuous James' situation was. When we went out for dinner, Fr. Stefan reminded us that James was going to be fine. Through another miracle, we were later told that James' bilateral brain bleed had healed itself and that his prognosis was good.

For the next month we watched James grow and gain strength. We were able to hold him skin-to-skin and feed him a bottle. Breast milk was supplemented with formula. The kids at school would hear about how all five of James' fingers were the same size as the top third of their finger and that his whole foot was smaller than the top half of their thumb. My prayers for Jesus to hold James continued.

In mid November, we went to MCV and, to our horror, found James' room empty. There was no incubator, no machines, nothing. Frantically, I questioned the nurses about the location of my son. They informed me that he had made the transition from the NICU to the Intermediate Care Unit, or Step-down Unit.

After Thanksgiving, we were told that once James was able to be off all monitors for fifteen days, he would be able to come home.

James was taken off monitors in early December. We were hoping to have James home for Christmas, but it appeared that it would be early January before he could come home. To our surprise, on December 14, we were notified that James would be released the following day. His bilateral brain bleed had resolved itself, and he was looking great. The hemangiomas were still large and quite evident, about the size of a half dollar, and protruding about one inch from his skull and leg.

Susan and I were sent into a separate room to learn how to use the home monitor and to psychologically prepare for caring for James at home. The nurses were across the hall ready to assist us. We were supposed to stay overnight, but we actually only spent four hours at the hospital. Early that evening we finally left the hospital with our little miracle in our arms.

It was a balmy December day when our kindergarten daughter would be performing in the Christmas show. Our pediatrician said it would be fine to take James to school. When we entered the gym, the room stood still. We had brought our miracle to share with all the people who had prayed for us and prepared home-cooked meals for us for the past fifty days. James was a living sign that Jesus was present not only at Christmas, but every day in their prayers and thoughts.

James is now four and has had a few encounters with potential illnesses (mainly in the first winter, as his body developed) As I write this, he is an intelligent, healthy, and very well developed four-year-old. He has no noticeable effects of his prematurity and has a wonderful head of brown hair that hides any remnants of his hemangioma. We still know it is there. That is where Jesus was holding him, pressing his face against James' head and removing any brain bleed.

Our little boy would not be alive if not for some gifted medical professionals. However, the true saving of his life was the result of many prayers and a great deal of unyielding faith, the faith that was started when he was baptized and God took him under his care.

EMILY'S STORY

by Theresa Rousseau

Emily came into the world on February 20, 2003 at 3:00 in the afternoon — the hour of mercy. She was three weeks early and weighed six pounds. Shortly after birth, we were told that Emily had Trisomy 21, better known as Down syndrome. Our immediate prayer was for her health, as we knew that babies with Down syndrome face many health challenges, especially heart problems. After a few days and many tests, we were told that Emily's heart was in good condition and she could go home.

Babies with Down syndrome are usually very sleepy due to their low muscle tone. They tend to have large tongues which make breastfeeding difficult, but since the benefits of breastfeeding outweigh the costs, we decided to breastfeed her. Although I nursed her every two hours, at two weeks of age her weight had dropped to five pounds, thirteen ounces, and the doctors were concerned.

Her doctor's visits became a daily occurrence as her weight was monitored. At three weeks, she still had not gained any weight, so the doctor ordered a series of blood tests. The tests showed that Emily had a rare form of jaundice and more tests were ordered to check out her liver. Nothing showed up, however, but at four weeks Emily had still not gained any weight. The doctor was concerned that she was now malnourished.

We were sent to MCV Hospital to see a specialist in blood disorders, and more blood tests were performed. This time, an answer was found. Emily was diagnosed with a rare form of childhood leukemia, resulting in a non-functioning liver. She needed to be hospitalized as soon as possible.

On the way home that day, my husband and I almost simultaneously said, "Let's go see Fr. Stefan." Fr. Stefan had recently been transferred to our old parish. We had heard him speak of healing and an incident where he prayed over a very sick infant who was consequently miraculously healed. We stopped by the church and Father was there. He didn't really know us, but he listened to our story and immediately prayed over Emily.

A few days later, Emily was admitted to the hospital where a nutrition program was established and her chemotherapy started. Our poor little Emily was so thin that the only place an IV could be placed was in her head.

At the end of the first round of chemo, the results were not good. There was no improvement in her leukemia, and her liver was still not functioning. A second round of chemo was ordered, but this time we were to administer it at home. Emily was discharged, and on the way home, we stopped again to see Fr. Stefan and have him pray over our little baby.

The next few weeks became a blur of blood tests, chemotherapy, blood transfusions, blood counts, and visits to Fr. Stefan. He prayed very intently over Emily, often in tongues, and he helped us to overcome our fears with a renewed faith in God and God's desire to heal.

At the end of the second round of chemo, we received some good news — Emily had gained weight, and her blood count numbers were good, indicating that the leukemia was gone. However, mixed with the good news was the bad news. Emily's liver was still not functioning; those numbers remained unchanged. Emily's doctor sat me down and said, "I know you are a praying woman. You really need to pray now. Emily cannot live without a functioning liver."

A third round of chemotherapy was ordered. We prayed and Fr. Stefan prayed, offering a healing Mass for my little girl. At the end of the third round of chemo, Emily's liver started to work. Praise God and his miracle of healing through the faith and prayers of Fr. Stefan!

Emily, now five years old, is a vibrant, high-functioning little girl who brings love, joy, and laughter — and Christ's presence — into our hearts and home every day. Praise God!

LET THE CHILDREN
COME UNTO ME

by Stephen P. Markle

I am very grateful to Fr. Stefan for the role he played in my conversion to the Catholic Faith. I was raised in a loving Christian family and indoctrinated with a strong belief in Our Lord Jesus Christ and all his miraculous works. My introduction to Catholicism came during preparation for the Sacrament of Matrimony to my wife, Patricia.

Through regularly attending Mass with my wife over the years, I gradually came to understand the differences between Protestant beliefs and the importance of the traditions of the Catholic Church. I finally decided to attend RCIA (Rite of Christian Initiation of Adults) classes with the goal of conversion. For various reasons, I was not able to follow through with the plan, and the idea of conversion was set aside. All that changed when Fr. Stefan baptized our son, John Samuel ("Sam").

Sam's first year was very difficult. When Patricia was seven months pregnant with him, we were in a traffic accident caused by an inattentive driver. The other vehicle hit us from behind while we were stopped at a stoplight. Patricia was in the driver's seat and forced against the steering wheel and jerked against her seatbelt. Although she felt fine, the next day she was advised to see her doctor for a "just-in-case" check up.

Attentive doctors found an alarmingly high abnormal baby heartbeat. During a routine exam just three days prior, Patricia and baby were given a clean bill of health, yet now a very irregular infant heartbeat was evident. At first, doctors suggested prenatal surgery might be warranted; at that time, however, one of the premier neonatal surgeons in the country was briefly assigned to the hospital. He advised monitoring the baby on a daily and, eventually, weekly basis in hopes that the condition would resolve independently. Fortunately, through God's grace, by the time Sam was born, his serious heart defect had repaired itself.

Sam was born at 6:25 a.m., August 10, 2000. Mother and baby passed all the tests and were released two days later. The next day, however, when Patricia checked on a napping Sam, she discovered a limp baby with a pronounced blue complexion. When she quickly lifted him up, Sam made a gasping noise. We called the pediatrician, who advised us to take Sam to an emergency room for evaluation.

The attending physician told Patricia that Sam had likely stopped breathing only moments before discovery. In the emergency room, the physician noted the baby had blue coloration of the skin when excited or agitated. The doctor suggested it was probably an isolated incident and advised us not to worry. However, during a well-baby visit on August 25, Patricia discussed the recent events with the doctor and similar observations of the condition were noted. Shortly thereafter, while being treated for a cold, Sam was given a consultation to an Ear, Nose, and Throat (ENT) Clinic.

On September 20, Sam was diagnosed with a condition that occurs when throat cartilage that supports the windpipe is not fully formed and allows the windpipe to close. For an infant like Sam, this meant certain head movements collapsed the windpipe, thus depriving him of oxygen. Some babies outgrow the condition; others require surgery to correct it. On subsequent visits, Sam displayed no real improvement. This led the doctor to recommend surgical intervention. A date for the somewhat risky surgery was scheduled.

Given the gravity of the situation, Patricia called the church and requested an emergency baptism prior to surgery. Alerted to Sam's condition, Fr. Stefan not only baptized Sam in the traditional manner, but he additionally sprinkled holy water on his throat while praying for God's healing grace.

Several days later, we returned to the clinic for the preoperative consult. During this examination, no trace of the condition was found, and the operation was cancelled.

While there may be several explanations for Sam's cure, I choose to believe God healed Sam using Fr. Stefan's hands as His tool and the holy water as a catalyst. This is the only explanation that matches the evidence: A sick little boy in need of surgery one day is completely healed the next. Our abiding faith leads us to believe God chose to perform a true miracle through Fr. Stefan.

On a personal note, I took this as a clear sign to renew my faith through becoming a member of the Catholic Church. Sometime later, I stopped Fr. Stefan while he was on a bike path. In thanking him, I mentioned that this event was the catalyst for my conversion and that our family remains filled with gratitude. This miracle truly changed my life and has given me profound, lasting peace. We are deeply thankful for Fr. Stefan's presence and special blessing that fateful day.

THE POWER OF THE KEYS

by Sam Pritchett

For years, I had held a sense of responsibility about my father's suicide. Though I was only a year old when it occurred, I was compelled to believe that maybe if I didn't cry as much, or if I smiled more, he would have been happier to stay with us. Dwelling incessantly upon that past led me into a deep depression with general anxiety. I kept it all to myself until the day it went overboard, and I felt coerced to end it all.

I went to retrieve the key to the gun cabinet and finish what God had begun: my life. As I reached for where the key was usually placed, it was missing. I searched the house frantically, and it still was nowhere to be found. It was the first miracle — God telling me, "No!"

Nevertheless, I was still in my trance and convinced that I must die. That's when I came across some pills. Consuming 2,400 milligrams of Zoloft, I finally snapped out of it and realized that what I was doing was not what I wanted. I turned to the phone and asked a friend to just "pray for me." Knowing that there was something more — since I was calling so early in the morning — he urged me to tell him what was going on. Finally, I opened up to him and he called the paramedics, who saved my life.

From the hospital, I was transferred to a mental institution. For a week and a half, I was stuck between locked doors, even missing my sister's First Communion. Then one night, I received a call from Fr. Stefan. He explained to me that suicide was a permanent answer to a temporary problem, and that he knew that God had something extraordinary for me to do in the future.

I finally returned home where things only became worse. At night, I began seeing shadows of demons everywhere within my room. And it didn't stop there. I noticed that they were not only in my room, or in my house, but everywhere I went. It was as if they wanted me. They were so frightening that they made me paranoid and caused panic attacks two to three times a day.

When I told Fr. Stefan about the demons, as soon as we could, Fr. Stefan and I scheduled a house blessing. He blessed the house, and later that night the demons truly wanted revenge. There were millions of them outside, inside, everywhere. I felt one go inside of me, and within me it tried to force me to choke myself. I ordered it to get out and declared that I was a daughter of God, then fell asleep praying the Rosary.

Fr. Stefan wanted me to have an intergenerational healing Mass, which is the healing of the family tree. He believed that there were some curses within my family history and wanted to rid us of them all. After a long, thorough praying of the maternal and paternal sides fifteen generations back, we saw another miracle from God. When Father reached into his pocket and pulled out his keys, one of his keys was bent!

Not only was the bent key a sign that Jesus was watching over me when I couldn't find the key to the gun safe, but that day the Gospel reading was about Jesus giving Peter the power of the keys to bind and loose. Fr. Stefan said the power of the keys is the power to bind and loose Satan. We, he and I both, believe that this bent key was a sign that I would obtain healing, and we all rejoiced at the work of God.

Later that night, at home, a cathartic anger and hatred expelled from me; as I looked around, I did not see dark shadows, but pure white ones. The next day I thanked God and opened the Bible up at random. My finger fell upon Mark 7:29, "And he said to her, 'For this saying you may go your way; the demon has left your daughter.'" Since that day, I still feel the healing power of God and am full of elation and joy. I truly give my thanks to God.

WILL YOU SUFFER FOR THE LOVE OF ME?

by Michelle Boardway

My story begins while being stationed overseas in Iwakuni, Japan. I worked as a teller at one of the banks on a military base. On a January day, I was not feeling well. I had a tremendous headache, my eye wouldn't stop twitching, and I felt dizzy and tired. My manager let me leave my post so I could go to the clinic. I saw the doctor on call. He checked all my reflexes and said everything was fine and sent me home.

I lay down and took a nap, and my husband picked up our son from daycare. I later got up and prepared dinner. During dinner my husband made a joke, and I started to laugh. Then he started to laugh and told me to stop making funny faces. I asked him, "What funny faces?"

He said, "Stop right there and go look in the mirror." To my horror, the whole left side of my face was paralyzed. Obviously, at that point my condition had become serious.

We returned to the clinic and the same doctor was on duty. He saw us come in and asked if I was still not feeling well. I responded, "No!" as I showed him my paralyzed face. He immediately did more reflex tests. He called the neurologist in Yokosuka, and together they recommended a battery of blood tests. The results indicated Bell's Palsy. They scheduled me for an MRI.

Since my eye wouldn't shut, I had to wear a patch to keep it from drying out. I could only drink out of a straw. I drooled. It was terrible. I remember having a conversation with my mother about how I didn't want to go back to work. She told me to pull myself up by my boot strings, and get moving. I had nothing to be

111

ashamed of. On my end of the phone I was mouthing, "Only my face, for Pete's sake." I couldn't even cry out of one eye. What's a girl to do if she can't even cry?

I went back to work. I was the taunt of people's jokes, especially of one girl who purposely tried to make me laugh so she could see my distorted face and point it out to the customers. I dreaded going to work.

A few weeks later, when I was visiting with my doctor, my lab results came in. He told me that I had what is called an autoimmune disease. Instead of the cells protecting the body, they attack the body. He wanted to test me for lupus, Lyme disease, rheumatoid arthritis, leukemia, and other diseases, as all of them could result in positive indicators of autoimmune disease.

I had the tests, and they all came back negative. Praise God! However, I still tested positive for the autoimmune disease. The doctor explained that some people test positive and some symptoms may not show up for years. For some people, they may never appear. Until the patient becomes symptomatic, doctors cannot diagnose a specific disease.

I walked out of the doctor's office knowing I had this disease that was invading my body, but they couldn't pinpoint what specific illness I had, so I couldn't be treated. They gave me this news and then said, "Just wait." It was very discouraging.

After a few days of sorting out my feelings of unfairness that I had Bell's palsy, an autoimmune disease, and that I was so far away from home, I looked at my little boy. He didn't care what I looked like. And every day, my husband sat patiently and listened to me as I related my embarrassing moments of taunting and my insecurities about my appearance. Through it all, he loved me just the same, if not more. He took care of me each night by putting drops in my eye and patching my eye shut. Then he would kiss me and tell me he loved me.

We laughed and joked about my condition because a few days before the Bell's palsy was fully evident, we were at Bingo Night and I didn't realize that my left eye wasn't shutting all the way. Each time I blinked, my husband's best friend, Steve, thought I was winking at him, and he was afraid to tell my husband. When the paralysis occurred a few days later, Steve understood my "winking." Among friends, this incident became a favorite joke and the cause of much laughter.

My Bell's palsy got better over time. I didn't fully recover — my left eye still droops a little, and my smile is still a little crooked — but no one notices except me. I would say that it improved about 98 percent. God is good.

As the years went on, I continued to be tested for autoimmune disease. I had started to experience a lot of aches and pains throughout my entire body, sometimes to the point where it was unbearable to the touch. Doctors prescribed Prednisone and painkillers to get me through the flare-ups. The test results always came back the same — positive for autoimmune disease, but no specific disease.

In September of 2006, Fr. Stefan Starzynski celebrated a healing Mass. After the Mass, when it was my turn to be prayed over, he called me up to the altar in front of the tabernacle. He laid his hands over me, and immediately I was slain in the Spirit. As I lay there, all I could see was a warm white glow. I experienced profound peace and I felt extraordinarily safe. Then I heard a voice say to me, "Will you suffer for the love of me?"

I knew exactly who was speaking to me. I responded, "Yes, as long as you hold my hand." At that very instant a sharp piercing pain, as if from a knife, went through my stomach. The pain was so great that I almost couldn't breathe. I sat straight up. At the healing Mass and prayer service, I usually stay for the entire service, but this night I was sobbing so uncontrollably and I was in such intense pain that I needed to leave immediately to get home.

A few days later, my arms and legs were racked with intense pain. This pain would continue. I didn't mention the pain to anyone until I saw my family doctor in November. She really couldn't do much for me except give me some medication to get me through the painful bouts. I followed up with her again in December.

In December 2006, as my condition worsened, the doctor sent me for blood tests. They ran the antibody test again, and again it was positive. This time the results were a little more elevated than in the past. The doctor thought it would be a good time for me to see a neurologist. They made my appointment for January. I looked up the neurologist on the Internet and found out that he was considered to be one of the best. I felt confident that I would be in good hands.

Christmas Day that year was an especially painful day for me. I remember that after opening the gifts and finishing Christmas dinner, my legs suddenly began to ache tremendously, to the point where I couldn't even walk or stand in the shower. We had made plans to go to a friend's house that evening for dessert. There was no way I was going to be able to go, so I told my family to go without me. I lay on the couch and cried. Then I stopped, realizing that it was a blessing to have time alone with the Lord on His birthday, even though I was in intense pain.

Three weeks passed, and the day of my appointment with the neurologist arrived. While we were driving into the parking lot of the hospital, I heard a voice say to me, "Will you suffer for the love of me?" Again, I knew exactly who was speaking to me.

I answered, "Yes, as long as you hold my hand." While we were walking into the hospital, the voice said again, "Will you suffer for the love of me?" I responded with the same answer.

While we were there, we met with the neurologist. He reviewed my entire medical history and then sent me to the lab for the blood work. As I was sitting there waiting for my blood to be drawn, the voice came back to me and asked me the same question eight more times, "Will you suffer for the love of me?"

I responded the same way all eight times, "Yes, because I know you will hold my hand." Then as my blood was being drawn, the voice again asked me the same question six more times. Responding the same way — but annoyed because my blood was being taken — I said, "Yes, because I know you will hold my hand." I then decided to pose my own question, "How many times are you going to ask me?" I never heard a response.

On January 18, 2007, a woman from church — just an acquaintance — rushed into the rectory office where I worked and handed me a framed picture of Our Lady of Guadalupe. She said, "Don't ask me why, but you are meant to have this picture right now," and then she was gone. It was the same picture that Evelyn James had had with her when Paul Stefan was born.

A few hours later I came home from work, and there was a message on my machine. It was from the neurologist, asking me to please give him a call. I thought, "Oh, this can't be good." So I took the picture I had received that day, kissed it, and said, "I guess this is why you are with me now."

I called the neurologist back, but was told that he was in a meeting until 2:30 p.m. The nurse said he would call me back. I asked the nurse if she could give me the results of my blood work because they hadn't been sent to my primary doctor who had been waiting for them. She told me that she didn't feel comfortable giving me the results and would prefer that the doctor speak with me.

I waited about two hours and finally received a call back from another nurse telling me that the doctor had to leave but he wanted to tell me that all my blood work came back normal. I asked in amazement, "Normal, as in I don't have any autoimmune disease?"

She said, "No, you don't." I asked her to immediately fax my results to my doctor.

I called my regular doctor at home that night. In addition to her knowing me medically, she knows me spiritually, since we go to the same church. I told her about my experience of hearing and answering Jesus' question at the healing Mass in September and hearing and answering his same question at the hospital. I asked her if she would inquire if the hospital used the same tests as everyone else. I told her that if they used the same tests that all the other medical facilities had used, then the change in the results indicated a miracle.

The following morning my doctor called me at work and asked if I was sitting down. Then she retorted, "Of course, you're sitting down." She had called the lab, and they confirmed that they had conducted the same tests as all the other facilities during the past seventeen years. The doctor could not explain how my autoimmune disease was now gone, since three weeks before, the test results had all been positive.

I have since been retested several times, and the results remain negative. I have spoken to various doctors and nurses, and they all say that it is highly uncommon for someone to have an autoimmune disease and then for it to just disappear, especially in three weeks' time, without a trace. I say nothing is impossible with God. "Yes, I will suffer for the love of you, because I know you will hold my hand."

"EYE HAS NOT SEEN . . ."

by Susan Wallace

In May 2007, my eyes itched. I had some tearing and blurry vision. Thinking it was allergies, I visited my ophthalmologist. After an examination, she prescribed medication and immediately ordered a complete blood workup. The results revealed that I had contracted the Epstein-Barr Virus (EBV), resulting in an inflammation of my eyes and entire digestive system. Untreated, EPV leads to chronic fatigue and other diseases because it reduces the effectiveness of the immune system, making one susceptible to contracting any illness. It potentially takes one to two years to recover from EPV. In addition to my eye discomfort, I suffered severe stomach pains after I ate, since all nourishment left my digestive system within one to three hours or less.

Fr. Stefan came to celebrate a healing Mass at our church in September 2007. As he walked the aisles, he touched my shoulder. I felt a warm, burning sensation go through my system. By the end of the Mass, Fr. Stefan asked if there was someone present with the name Susan, and said, "You are healed." By the end of the month, my condition improved, and I was able to reduce the medications. My digestive system was now able to process and hold food properly and the stomach pains were also immensely reduced. Since I felt fine, I was released from the doctor's care.

In February 2008, a second more aggressive virus — cytomegalovirus, which causes inflammation of the retina and colon — severely affected my eyes, causing a hemorrhage in the cornea; once again, I restarted treatment. At Fr. Stefan's healing Mass in April, he said eyes were being cured. That night and the next day, I noticed an improvement in my vision and a lessening of the symptoms. A return to the doctor for a checkup in May confirmed there was no virus present. Once again, I was released from care.

HEALINGS

by Linda Zauzig

In the spring of 2007, I started having some female problems which resulted in a surgical procedure at the hospital. My health was fine until December of 2007, when exploratory procedures were undertaken to determine the cause of some bleeding.

On December 5, 2007, I was given the bad news that my endometrial lining was excessively thickened. I was immediately scheduled for an even more invasive procedure — a hystersonogram — the following week, in order for the doctors to view the uterus more clearly.

On December 8, 2007, my son Kevin attended Fr. Stefan's healing Mass. Kevin was not aware of the severity of my doctor visits; he only knew that I was scheduled for a medical procedure. Unbeknownst to me, Kevin stood in my stead and prayed for my healing.

On December12, 2007, the fourth day after the healing Mass and also the feast day of Our Lady of Guadalupe, I went in for my hystersonogram. My husband accompanied me, and we nervously watched the monitor as a probe viewed my uterus. The doctor was very quiet, not making many comments until he exclaimed, "Oh, there is a very tiny polyp." He stated that it was not big enough to cause any bleeding problems. It was so small that it had been undetectable on the previous sonogram. He measured my endometrial wall, and although I was very afraid to hear the answer, I asked, "What does it measure?" He answered very matter-of-factly, "Oh, it's a five — totally normal." I was flabbergasted! The week before it had been a ten — up two digits from the previous year, when it had been an eight.

At a measurement of eleven and up, doctors investigate for possible cancer. It was a five! It was normal! God had intervened for me and had physically healed me of a potentially life-threatening situation.

Over the next two months, I had very minor episodes of intermittent bleeding. On February 9, 2008, when I went to Fr. Stefan's healing Mass, I was not in search of healing for my physical well-being, but my emotional well-being. I had had to put down my beloved fourteen-year-old greyhound, Reason, on February 7, and I was much in need of an emotional healing. Once again, God blessed me in his undeniably-from-God fashion. He not only unburdened my heavy heart over the loss of my dog, but since that night I have not experienced any more bleeding. It is now seven months later.

God heals in the most wondrous ways. Even when I don't feel worthy of his blessings and graces, he continually surprises me with them. They are a constant reminder that he is always with me. He never leaves me. When I need him the most and when times are hardest, he guides me to what I need to hear, see, or feel in order to ease the pain. This is the ultimate gift of all — his love for me.

I told my friend Mary about my healing, and she told her daughter Katie, whose friend had colon cancer. We went to the healing Mass to pray for Katie's friend, and God answered our prayers for her, too.

GOD'S GOAL FOR JESS

by Mary Silverthorne

Katie's college field hockey teammates became her second family. Their coach attributed the team's unprecedented success to the group's palpable cohesiveness, on and off the turf.

Shortly after graduation, one teammate, Jess, was diagnosed with colon cancer. She had surgery and completed a grueling chemo regimen. She was thought to have beaten the dreaded disease — but then Jess' symptoms returned and persisted. After two diagnoses of irritable bowel syndrome (IBS), Jess sought a third opinion. It was a tearful doctor who contradicted the diagnoses of IBS, and informed Jess that she had Stage 4 colon cancer that had spread to her lungs, liver, and lymph nodes. Jess would begin another grueling chemo regimen.

Katie spent the next day surfing the Internet. She learned that Stage 4 colon cancer is a dire diagnosis. She approached me, because she knew my friend and I were attending a healing Mass the upcoming weekend. I was thrilled when she asked if she could come along.

At the end of the Mass, Katie explained that she had said a novena, and this was the day she was expecting a "sign." Katie really believed, so she was very disappointed because she hadn't received the sign. I told her that she might have missed it, that she had to be careful not to overlook it.

When I finished speaking, the look of delighted astonishment on her face was unmistakable. She asked, "Mom, can a song be a sign?"

Katie already knew the answer. She said that there were only two songs in the world that she could have heard at that moment that would have reminded her of her teammates, and the choir had just started singing one of them, "We Are One in the Spirit." The team's jokester used to sing this song while running up and down the aisle of the bus as the team traveled to away games.

As we approached the altar for our blessings, Fr. Stefan left the far side of the church, where he had been blessing people, and stood in the center of the altar. He said, "Who prayed for someone with cancer? Right now, someone is being healed of their cancer." As he uttered these words, he looked right at my daughter and me. It was as if he knew it was us. Being somewhat of a skeptic, I followed his eyes. They did not dart about to meet the eyes of the many, many people gathered there. His eyes stayed fixed on us.

The healing Mass was on a Saturday, and Jess was scheduled for a battery of tests over the next couple of days. To everyone's amazement, the tests confirmed that the treatment was working.

At last report, there was one small spot on Jess' liver, and the spot on her lung had shrunk. Though she sailed through all her previous chemo treatments, presently Jess is having a particularly difficult time. While radiological studies continue to be encouraging, side effects have necessitated that chemo dosages be adjusted.

One doctor commented to me that anyone with a Stage 4 colon cancer diagnosis has been given a death sentence; medical science has its limits. But God has no constraints. With God, anything is possible. His works defy imagination or explanation. We trust that God has a plan for Jess, and Jess is hoping to come to Virginia and accompany us to next month's healing Mass.

Jesus, we pray that you heal Jess, and we ask the Blessed Mother to intercede in the glory of her Son's name on behalf of Jess. Lastly, we thank you for all your blessings.

Amen.

SINGLE WHITE ROSE

by Kathy Mercer

In August 2001, I was diagnosed with leukemia. I had sought God's help in healing and had gone to various healing services. In 2004, Fr. Stefan was new to my mother's parish, and she wanted me to go to his healing Masses, so in the fall, I went. I still remember how I felt as Fr. Stefan placed his hands on my head and prayed over me. I felt a rush of heat that started at the top of my head and seemed to go through my entire body. I fell to the ground and lay there for a moment.

Shortly after, I had a blood test that showed my leukemia cells decreasing. In May 2005, my mother and I went to Medjugorje with Fr. Stefan. The blood test I had that summer showed that the leukemia cells were reduced even further.

Fr. Stefan had asked me to give a testimony at one of his healing Masses, but I asked God for a sign that I was to speak at the healing Mass. My sign would be that Fr. Stefan would ask me again. I figured he would forget, so that would be a reasonable request and sign. Then, he asked me again at the August 2005 healing Mass, and I felt that my request must have been too easy! So I asked God for another sign. This time, the sign was to be a single white rose that was specifically for me — not just one that I saw.

Two weeks later, I was outside pulling weeds. As I looked up, I saw a single white rose on what I thought was a dead rosebush. What was most telling though — this was a *pink* rosebush, not a white one!

In 2006, all my test results would show no signs of leukemia cells. How great is our God!

MIRACLE BABY

by Joanne McDonough

One day, Fr. Stefan came to our home to bring Holy Communion to my sick husband. While he was there, he told me it was his observation that I needed some relief from the 24/7 caretaking responsibilities. He suggested that I get some help and get out of the house from time to time.

I remember he had invited me to attend his healing Masses, which I decided to do. While at these Masses, I prayed that my daughter and I would have our prayers answered, that she would conceive a child after having been married for six years.

Subsequently, I arranged to place my husband in custodial care for two weeks and joined Fr. Stefan's pilgrimage to Medjugorje. While there, I requested the Blessed Mother to hasten the answer to our prayers. Two weeks after we returned from Medjugorje, my daughter called and said she was pregnant. Our miracle baby's name is Jordyn.

A SIGN FROM GOD

by Cathy Wester

I am employed at a Catholic Church, and it is my custom to come in early each morning before I start work to spend some time in prayer before the Blessed Sacrament. I was sitting in my usual spot in the chapel, sometime between the second and third healing Masses (August and September 2007) celebrated by Fr. Stefan at my parish, when I noticed a piece of paper by the tabernacle under the ablution cup (a vessel that is filled with water and used by those who distribute Holy Communion to purify their fingers of any sacred particles of the Host).

I got up to investigate. I removed the note and sat back down, placing the note on the chair beside me. After setting it on the chair, though, I kept thinking about it, so I decided to read it. It was a lovely note written to Jesus and Mary about some babies that had holes in their hearts and how they needed to be healed. I decided I would pass this on to the pastor.

I set the note back down, but again, my thoughts kept returning to it, and I got the inspiration to pray for the babies. I took the paper in my hands and prayed like I've never prayed before. I almost glanced around behind myself to see if anyone was looking, certain they would be able to read my mind.

I passed the note on as I had originally planned, and we never spoke of it, nor did I mention it to Fr. Stefan. At first I let go of the prayer request, but then I began to wonder how the babies were doing. I asked God to give me a sign. I asked him to let me know if my prayer made an impact on the babies' health.

On September 18, I came into work and sat in my usual spot in the chapel. I noticed another note up by the tabernacle, under the ablution cup. Again, I went up to investigate. The note read:

9-17-07

Thank you, merciful Savior, for healing the hearts of little Jackson and Dameon without surgery being needed!

Jim

When I read that note and realized it was an answer to my prayer, I was in awe. I felt that the note was from Jesus. To have received such a direct answer to prayer was overwhelming, but I am very grateful for it.

MY MIRACLE

by Felix Mestey

I believe in miracles. I know that some people consider an event a miracle only if it is something quite extraordinary that occurs in an instant. Yes, there are many miracles of this nature, but I believe that many other miracles also occur in a more subtle way. They happen in a gradual way; in the case of healing, many times not only is the body healed, but also the mind, and most importantly, the soul as well.

I am not sure when my ailment started. I know that I began experiencing some strange sensations in my eyes. Last year, 2007, in the month of July, I was driving behind my wife Vivian's minivan on our way to Washington, Georgia. Traveling with her were my two daughters, Vianlix and Vivian Christine, and my two grandkids. We had started early in the morning to get ahead of the rush-hour traffic. The morning was nice and cool, so I decided to roll my windows down, even after I got onto the interstate.

I was very excited. This was our second trip to Washington, Georgia, and it would be the last one planned to finish filming the second part of a movie that my younger daughter, Vianlix, had written, cast, produced, and directed. This project was a family venture. We had formed a film corporation with a very limited budget. All the actors were volunteers — friends and relatives. Vianlix had been rehearsing with them for the past two years in order to transform them into actors.

The past two years had been quite rough for all of us, not so much because of the movie project but because of the breast cancer diagnosis, treatment, and recovery of my older daughter, Vivian. Now fully recovered — yes, a miracle — Vivian was traveling with her son in the car in front of me. She was full of health and as happy as one can be in this great world that God has given to us.

About four hours into the trip, I decided to roll up my car's windows. Although it was now warm and more humid, the main reason that I rolled up the windows was because I felt a burning sensation in both eyes, but it was stronger in my left eye. Even with the windows up, it got worse as time passed.

The next day in Washington, Georgia, I went to see an ophthalmologist. His diagnosis was that I was most probably suffering from an acute case of allergies caused by exposing myself to pollen or some other contaminant the day before. He prescribed two different kinds of eye drops and told me that he expected they would take care of my problem. However, they didn't, at least not for my left eye. We continued to work long hours filming; most days, more than fifteen hours. My left eye continued to get worse. After two weeks, I was unable to drive back to Virginia. Upon my return home, I went to see a local ophthalmologist.

When my older daughter became ill with breast cancer, our family would gather for prayer. As a family, we prayed the Rosary daily, as well as weekly with friends. We visited the San Pio Center in Barto, Pennsylvania, and the Fatima Center in Washington, New Jersey, several times. We learned, and lived, one of Padre Pio's ten rules to get closer to God: When you have a problem that you want God to help you solve, there is a simple way, You pray, hope, and do not worry. Mary also taught us of her motherly love to intercede for us with Jesus, her Son, to accept God's will, and to be patient.

We did all these things for my daughter during her illness and it worked, so we started doing the same for me in my ailment. Even when my condition appeared to worsen, I had confidence in Jesus Christ's love for me and knew that he would take care of me. This gave us all strength, and we found it easy to give ourselves over to his will.

For three months, the local ophthalmologist continued to treat me with many different medicines and eye drops, including steroids — with potential serious side effects — but the condition continued to worsen. A growth formed above the left eye, where the tear gland is located. It was quite large and was crushing my cornea, causing me to have double vision. By the third month, after I had seen several doctors — an internist, a neurologist, and an allergist — and had numerous blood tests, X-rays, an MRI, and a CT scan, most possible causes were discarded.

The allergist rejected the idea that it was an allergy and insisted I see an ophthalmologist at the Johns Hopkins Hospital. With all the specialists in one place, they would be able to diagnose my problem more effectively. Although I had picked this allergist from the telephone directory and this was the first appointment, he called an ophthalmologist colleague at Johns Hopkins and got me a medical appointment for the following week. What made him call? I believe that God was using the allergist as part of his miracle in the making.

In September 2007, I was seen by a group of ophthalmologists, who immediately suspected cancer and referred me to a plastic surgeon specializing in eyes. This world-renowned specialist was in the building at that time and was available to see me after a full day of surgeries. He joined the team of four doctors who decided that I needed a biopsy of the growth over my left eye. Two weeks later, the biopsy was performed. A week later, I was given the diagnosis of lymphoma on top of my left eye. I continued the prayers, my hope in God, and the "don't worry" approach.

I was then referred to an oncologist specializing in lymphoma at Johns Hopkins. He indicated that if the cancer was just on my eye, I could be given an innovative treatment of the immune system, along with radiation over the tumor. Although the treatment would delay the advancement of the cancer for several years, the radiation could eliminate the tumor.

Eastern Europe had confirmed cases of such lymphomas as mine in people who had been in close proximity with birds, or who had been exposed to a common bacteria, *chlamydia psitacci*, carried by some birds and released in their droppings. These patients had responded well to a regimen of antibiotics. He cautioned me that there were no studies of how effective this treatment was, nor if the lymphomas could recur. After seeing me, he sent me to have a PEP scan of my whole body to check if the cancer had spread.

After a few weeks, I saw the oncologist to discuss the PEP scan results. He indicated that the scan had confirmed that the growth over the left eye was indeed a lymphoma, and it also had identified other possible spots in my chest as well. That being that the case, he would not use radiation because of the risk of damage to my eye.

Remembering what he said about the birds, I mentioned that when I was a boy I used to go to a farm to visit a friend and we played among the cocks and chickens. I also told him that when I was about twelve years old, we kept some chickens in my yard. Hearing that, he recommended that we try the innovative treatment of the immune system, that we had nothing to lose in trying the regimen of antibiotics. He prescribed doxycycline, a commonly used antibiotic for treating malaria, for three weeks. I continued the prayers, my hope in God, and the "don't worry" approach.

I could literally see the tumor over my eye receding after just the first week of treatment. By the end of the third and last week of treatment, the tumor was reduced by about 70 percent. When I saw the oncologist, he indicated that he had not seen such a remarkable remission before. He ordered another PEP scan to check the status of what has been detected in my chest.

Before I went for the second PEP scan, I attended Fr. Stefan's healing Mass. That day Fr. Stefan indicated that he got a message about the healing of someone in the church suffering from eye cancer. Moved by his sermon and the charismatic Mass, and with my eye tumor and the double vision gone, I gave testimony of my healing. I mentioned that I was scheduled for a second PEP scan to check for the potential lymphoma that the previous PEP scan had shown in my chest.

After several other testimonies of healing along with mine, I stood with many others around the altar. For the first time in my life I received the Holy Spirit when Fr. Stefan prayed over me and touched my head. I felt a peace that I had never experienced before.

A week after the Mass, I went for the second PEP scan. Two weeks later, the oncologist told me that nothing was detected in my eye, my chest, or in any other part of my body. He could not explain what had happened — but I could. I had received God's healing, a miracle.

I was later called by Johns Hopkins personnel asking for details of my case; it was then used in a conference presentation to the students and professors of the medical school and doctors on their staff. My case is the only known one in the world where a complete remission has been documented for this type of lymphoma.

By the end of August, I had a follow-up CT scan and a follow-up appointment with the oncologist. For the doctors it was hard to understand what had happened. For those with faith, it was clear: a miracle had happened, and I had been healed. I continue the prayers, my hope in God, and the "don't worry" approach.

YOU WILL NEVER HAVE CANCER AGAIN

by Patti Chehovin

At my third healing Mass, in March 2008, I was praying for family members — specifically for my dad, who had gone through chemotherapy a few years ago to fight non-Hodgkin's lymphoma. My mom feared that his cancer was returning because she and Dad had discovered more lesions on his head and neck.

During the Mass, I looked up at the statue of the risen Christ and felt as though Jesus was saying to me, "Your father will never have cancer again." With eyebrows raised and jaw dropped, I looked to my left and then to my right. I slowly turned back to the statue of Christ, and I heard even more clearly, "Your father will never have cancer again!" Fairly rattled, I thought, *Is this just me wishing and hoping? Or is this really you, Lord, speaking to me?*

At that exact moment in the Mass, Fr. Stefan said, "Friends, we're at a *healing Mass*. If you get a word or a message, *trust* that it's from the Lord." That was exactly what I needed to hear to believe that the message I received was truly from God.

The next day, I called my dad and shared the incredible message from God that I had received at the healing Mass. My dad believed. Weeks later, when Dad got his biopsy results, his doctor confirmed what we already knew: My dad does not have cancer. Thank you, Lord!

THE CANCER IS GONE

by Dennis Downham

On June 12, 2006, I was diagnosed with kidney cancer. By August 9, 2006, my right kidney and a small part of my bladder were removed. This surgery led to numerous follow-up appointments with my doctor. Each time, non-invasive cancer was found in my bladder and scraped away.

In March 2007, after one of my checkups, I was told the cancer had become embedded in my bladder and prostate, and I was going to lose both organs. My doctor said he had already consulted with a cancer specialist and he agreed that both organs had to be removed.

During this process, my church, Calvary Road Baptist Church — along with my family and many other churches in Virginia, Washington, DC, North and South Carolina, and Florida — had been praying for me. Then on April 22, 2007, I was at my sister's home celebrating her granddaughter's baptism, when I met Fr. Stefan. While at my sister's home, Fr. Stefan anointed my two brothers and me with St. Joseph's oil and prayed over each of us.

On April 30, 2007, I underwent a more intensive procedure to retrieve more biopsies to see if any other organs were affected. When my wife and I met with the doctor one week later to schedule surgery, he said it was nothing he had done, but the cancer was gone.

HEALING MASSES

by Dee Hazard

Fr. Stefan had invited me to his healing Masses many times, but I always told him, "No, thank you. I'm not charismatic." Very early one morning, I was in church when Fr. Stefan approached me and said he was praying for my back. This startled me because I had never told anyone it bothered me. It was just very painful, but I thought a doctor would only recommend surgery. I didn't want to do that, so it was something I lived with and "offered it up."

When I asked him how he knew there was anything wrong, he didn't answer that question but said he wanted me to attend the healing Mass that weekend. After thinking about it extensively, I decided to go. After Mass, Father prayed over me, and by the next morning, all the pain I had experienced for a number of years had disappeared. Over the past couple of years, it has never returned. I now believe in and attend healing Masses.

MARY'S ROSE

by Wenda Pancotti

Mary began her devotion to St. Thérèse of Lisieux when she was about seven or eight years old. She told me she was praying for roses from St. Thérèse. I was making her a dress for Halloween and told her that the roses on the material for the dress could be the roses she had been praying for. She said, "No, I'm going to get real roses." We came home one evening and at the carport door was a box that said *Rose Express*. It was a dozen red roses that had been sent randomly as an advertising promotion. This began Mary's devotion to St. Thérèse.

Mary had cystic fibrosis and received a double lung transplant in September of 2005. In September of 2006 she developed lymphoma, and in 2007 a virus began destroying her kidneys. She developed a cancerous brain tumor in the late fall of 2007 and died on December 30, 2007, at the age of nineteen.

Two days before her death, while Mary was at dialysis, she told me that St. Thérèse of Lisieux was there with her. Mary referred to her as "St. Theresa" most of the time. She said, "Look, she is right over there," and pointed to the corner of the room. I asked Mary what she was saying and she said something that sounded French. She repeated it when I asked again what she had said. It sounded like "champin blanc."

I left because a family relative came in to stay with Mary while I went to eat and shower. She also told our friend that St. Thérèse was there with her. The Catholic chaplain, who had spent many hours with Mary over the years, came to visit while she was in dialysis. Mary told Sister that St. Thérèse was there, too. Sister came to the room to see me. She told me that she had been praying for St. Thérèse to bring Mary comfort. The family relative who was staying with her was there when Mary said that St. Thérèse had left. Mary then began singing *The First Noël*.

The next day, December 29, Mary was doing better. She was talking more, sitting up, walking, and her blood work was improved somewhat. I asked her about St. Thérèse. She responded, "Oh yes, I saw St. Theresa." I asked her what she looked like, and she said that she was more beautiful than anyone else in the hospital and she had the most straightened black hair she had ever seen. I then asked her if St. Thérèse had said anything to her. Mary told me that "St. Theresa" had told her, "Hi, God loves me, I'll be well, and I'm going home."

At Mary's graveside service on January 4, 2008, I was given a rose with a photograph of St. Thérèse by one of the Child Life specialists at the hospital. She had brought two roses and photographs, one for me and one to be left at the graveside for Mary. We put the one I was given in a vase in Mary's room when we got home. The rose opened fully and continued to stay beautiful for well over twenty-six days. Finally, on February 6, I took it to a local florist. It had spouted new growth on the stem and still had petals. As of this writing, six months later, the growth from the rose is still alive.

Mary had asked for a chocolate éclair about ten days before she died. We all asked her if she was sure, because chocolate éclairs were not something she had ever eaten. One of our friends brought her one, and one of Mary's friends cut it up and helped her to eat it. After Mary died, Rolando, her father, suggested that we watch the St. Thérèse movie to see if the French words were in there. There were no French words in the movie. However, in the book *The Last Conversations of St. Thérèse*, it's documented that St. Thérèse asked for and ate a chocolate éclair.

BELIEVE

by Vivian Mestey

In October 2007, I had my annual mammogram. The results were negative. However, during the procedure, the technician had put pressure on my armpit and soon thereafter, I felt constant pain in that area. Two weeks later I felt a small lump, but since my mammogram had been negative, I had peace of mind.

In January 2008, I went for my annual Pap smear and told the doctor about the pain that I was experiencing under my armpit. My OB-GYN is also an oncologist and knew of my family history of cancer. After she completed a physical examination of my armpit, her diagnosis was an ingrown hair. I felt confident in her diagnosis.

In March, I went back to the doctor; the diagnosis remained unchanged, but the doctor prescribed an antibiotic. In April, I went back for a third appointment, at which time we agreed that I should have another mammogram, and the doctor also ordered a sonogram as well. The results of the mammogram were not what I expected. The doctor now ordered a biopsy; the results came back positive. I had breast cancer.

This is where Fr. Stefan enters the story. My friend Veronica told me about Fr. Stefan's healing Mass. I went to the healing Mass and received the Holy Spirit, and I experienced enormous joy when Fr. Stefan prayed over me. In the days following the Mass, I underwent more tests to see if the cancer had spread. The following week I received the PET/CT results. They were negative! Even after six months with an incorrect diagnosis and no treatment, the cancer had not spread. This was a miracle.

At the second healing Mass, when Fr. Stefan prayed over me, I received another outpouring of the Holy Spirit. The medical outcomes after that Mass were incredible. I went through my first treatment of chemotherapy with no side effects — absolutely none. This continued throughout the entire first round of four chemotherapy treatments.

At the next healing Mass, before Fr. Stefan prayed over me, I told him that I suffered from an anxiety disorder that could not even be successfully controlled with medication. Fr. Stefan prayed over me, and again I felt the power of the Holy Spirit. It's been two months now, and I have had no anxiety attacks. Another miracle!

I continued another round of chemotherapy treatments, and I still didn't suffer from side effects. At one point the nurse asked me, "Are you okay?" I told her that I was, and she responded, "This is awesome." She could tell I was doing well because she said I looked great. Another miracle!

After the four rounds of chemotherapy, I saw my surgeon when he wanted to do a physical evaluation. Because of the constant miracles, I knew that I had been healed. While the doctor was doing the examination, he looked at me and said, "It's gone. There is nothing there. It's gone!" The lymph nodes were gone! His smile was priceless. For me, it was the best blessing ever. Another miracle!

It's been a blessing to know Fr. Stefan. Fr. Stefan provided the words and wisdom I needed to hear — that Jesus wanted to heal me. This cross was too heavy to carry on my own, so faith and prayer carried it for me.

My family and I have survived five tsunamis, but we have also received personal healings through the power of faith. First, my daughter was healed from breast cancer, and then my husband's lymphoma in his left eye was healed. Next, my granddaughter was healed from a serious congenital heart defect, and fourth, when my other daughter went to have a biopsy of a lump in her breast, the doctor couldn't find it. He said, "It's gone." The fifth healing — but, I'm certain, not the last one in our lives — is my own healing of breast cancer and an anxiety disorder.

My daughter and I have created our own dictionary of meanings related to our diseases:

Breast Cancer: Before Christ
Red (color) Chemo: the Blood of Christ
Taking medication for five years: the Body of Christ
Believe: My personal mantra

I have committed my life to Jesus and to his Blessed Mother; I had prayed that I would live to give testimony to their loving kindness. My life has radically changed for the better. I may never know why I received these miracles, but I believe that everything has a purpose. If these illnesses and miracles have brought me where I am supposed to be spiritually, it's all been worth it.

Thank You, Fr. Stefan, for giving me hope and faith. Thank you for the long hours that you dedicate to us in praying over everyone in need. You have helped me to focus on the life that I want to live, a life dedicated to serving our Lord.

AN ANGEL

by Dawn Rizzoni

The healing Mass that my family and I attended last July just blew me away. I had never been to a healing Mass before and had no idea what to expect. I just brought my faith with me and went along for the ride.

At the end of the Mass, everyone was called to the altar for a blessing. The priest was speaking in tongues and people were actually falling to the ground. This was very strange for me. As a lifelong Catholic, I'd never seen anything like this and was a little uncomfortable. I watched one woman, though, next to us, as she started to fall. She truly looked startled, kind of laughing almost, and was trying to hold herself up, but she couldn't. She really looked surprised that she was falling. If you saw her on the street, you wouldn't think this was a woman who would want to fall to the ground in front of hundreds of people. She seemed very formal, very refined. When it came time for my husband, Rob, to be blessed, I really lost my composure. I, too, don't like to show too much emotion in public, but audible sobs were coming out of me. I was praying to God that this would be Rob's miracle, the one we'd been waiting for. The strange thing was that, right before Fr. Stefan got to my husband, he stopped his blessings, went up to the altar, and said, "Someone is going to be healed of cancer." Then, he returned to my husband.

Because cancer (an abnormal cytology study and a growth in his prostate) was still a possibility for my husband, I wondered if Fr. Stefan was referring to him when he made this statement. How odd that Father said this right before blessing Rob. My son was next in the line to be blessed; he's only ten, and he was shaking. After Father had blessed him, he sat down with my husband and started crying uncontrollably. "I didn't even know I was going to cry," he said later. "I didn't even know it was coming. It just came out of me."

I moved my daughter Natalie in front of me, saying to Fr. Stefan, "My whole family needs a blessing!" He put his hands on my head instead, looked into my eyes, and asked me what my name was.

I had not seen him speak to anyone else while doing this, other than to pray or speak in tongues. I told him my name, and he then asked if I went to St. Mary of Sorrows. I said no and told him where we were from. Then he said, "Relax," so I closed my eyes. Next, he said, "Believe." And I did believe. Faith is one thing that I am definitely full of!

"I see an angel coming toward you," he continued. "I see the angel surrounding you. Everything is going to be okay."

I burst into tears at that point and he finished the blessing. I didn't fall down, though, and I almost was envious of those who did. Was I less holy, less worthy? Why didn't that happen to me?

I remember Father saying, though, not to go by your feelings. The Holy Spirit works in different ways in different people, he said, and you might not feel anything at all.

I then remembered someone telling me once that crying is a sign that the Holy Spirit is moving through you. And it hit me then that, although I didn't fall, the tears that flowed so copiously from my eyes, and from Matthew's eyes, were from the Holy Spirit. The Spirit was with us and in us.

And to be told that an angel is surrounding you and making sure everything's going to be okay! Priceless. My husband and I always try so hard to hold our family together through all of our health crises.

Now, whenever things seem to be at their worst, and I feel like I can't handle one more thing, I'm going to remember that an angel is by my side.

We went to McDonald's for dinner after the Mass that evening, and the guy who took our payment had a nametag on that said "Rafael." Our angel? You decide.

FAITH THE SIZE OF A MUSTARD SEED

by Iris Ryan

Matthew 17:20 tells us, "For truly, I say to you, if you have faith as a grain of mustard seed, you will say to this mountain, 'Move hence to yonder place,' and it will move; and nothing will be impossible to you."

A mustard seed is indeed very little, measuring only one-six-teenth of an inch long. Surely, I thought to myself, I could have enough faith the size of one mustard seed, at the very least.

I had suffered from stomach problems since the birth of my first child almost fourteen years before. I'd gone to various doctors and a couple of gastroenterologists, and although most were help-ful and tried treating my symptoms, I never fully recovered. My only relief was to keep to a strict gluten and dairy-free diet.

When I first heard Fr. Stefan preach at our church, he spoke about the healings of various people and holding healing Masses. I listened intently and hoped that I, too, could be healed. I knew that God might desire for me to "carry my cross" — that is, my stomach sensitivities — but I knew that there was also hope that he might desire for me to be healed completely. I spoke to Fr. Stefan after the Mass and asked him what I needed to do. He said I could be healed by him praying over me right then and there. He prayed with me right there after Mass. I didn't try to eat wheat or dairy right away, and my stomach did not appear to get better or worse.

Later, I heard about the healing Mass and knew I had to attend with my family. After the Mass, Fr. Stefan went to each person individually and prayed over them, asking the Holy Spirit to come and heal them. Some people were falling slowly backward (someone was prepared to catch them and lay them gently on the carpet). My son and husband looked at me as though this was a bit too strange, but I didn't mind. In fact, I wished that when it was my turn I would feel something and see a visible sign, such as falling to the ground. I prayed that God would increase my faith.

When it was my turn for prayers, Fr. Stefan prayed, "Let the joy come out of the stomach, Lord." He repeated this phrase and then spoke in tongues. My eyes were closed and I was praying for healing. I thought I saw a bright light with my eyes closed. The light felt warm and I fell gently to the ground. The light seemed to be around me, and I continued to pray with my eyes closed. I could hear my daughters' concerned voices around me, so I opened my eyes and stood up.

We went home, and I still didn't know if I had been healed. My daughters wanted me to try eating pizza or ice cream right away, but I hesitated. I wanted God's okay before I ate bread and dairy.

Later, Fr. Stefan asked me how I was feeling. I told him I hadn't tried eating bread or dairy yet. I knew all I needed was faith as big as a mustard seed. I told Fr. Stefan that I believed I already possessed that faith, though, as I recounted a story to him from my childhood:

We often lived paycheck to paycheck, and one day, my mother ran out of baby food for my little brother. She never nursed because she believed (as many did at the time) that store-bought food and formula milk were better for babies. We had checked all the cupboards, but we couldn't find a single jar of baby food.

My dad was getting paid that day, and soon he would get off of work and go to the store to buy groceries, but my baby brother was crying because he was hungry. My mom gathered all her children and prayed to God for help. When she was done praying, she instructed us saying, "Okay, now go look again." Even though we had all just finished looking, we went through the cupboards again. There, right in front, we saw a jar of banana baby food. My brother ate it and took a nap. By the time he woke, there was plenty of food that my dad had brought from the store. My mother taught me to have faith and to believe and hope in prayers.

When I saw Fr. Stefan at church a week later, he asked me if I had tried eating bread yet. "Not yet," I replied. At that, he pulled a tiny mustard seed out of his pocket and handed it to me, saying, "I think it's time for you to try eating some bread."

I thought of how the apostles all performed healings and other miraculous signs. I know that the Lord still heals people to this day. Perhaps he had healed me, I thought.

After avoiding bread and dairy for so long, it was rather difficult for me to even try a bit of bread, but I prayed that God would reveal to me what I could and couldn't eat so I could be healthy. That day, I tried a tiny bit (hardly a bite) of banana bread my mother had made. I felt fine afterward. The next day I tried a bigger bite. After a few days, I tried half a slice of bread, and worked up to one slice of bread. My stomach gradually felt better and better. Each day I was able to eat a little more than I could eat before the healing.

I was so thrilled to be able to eat bread again that I almost felt as if asking for a dairy tolerance as well would be a bit greedy. However, Fr. Stefan later asked me if I had tried eating ice cream again. After his promptings, I did try ice cream in an ice cream cake — a very little bit, and I was fine afterward. I do take Lactaid pills (which help in the digestion of dairy) whenever I eat dairy products and I limit dairy, but still it is so nice to be able to eat dairy again!

BE NOT AFRAID

by Chris Grzasko

Several years ago, Fr. Stefan discovered that I had never been on an airplane. Unlike him, I'm not much of a traveler. I had never ventured farther away from home than a two-day drive. Flying never appealed to me, and the thought of it actually made me quite apprehensive. But, upon learning of this qualm of mine, it became Fr. Stefan's mission to get me on a plane.

After I began working with him on writing this book, he surmised that the perfect ending for his book would be to get me to conquer my fear of flying. He told me that as an expression of his gratitude for all my work on the book, he wanted to purchase a plane ticket for me to travel anywhere I wanted in the United States.

He spent months asking me where I wanted to go. I did my best to avoid answering the question, since I was still uncomfortable with the idea of flying. About nine months into the project, we were at a dinner theater with some members of the Young Adult Group when he asked me again. I figured I couldn't avoid the question any longer. If I had to fly, I concluded that a short flight would be best. Some good friends of mine live in Atlanta, Georgia, and I had never been there to visit them. I told Fr. Stefan that I wanted to go to Atlanta. His response was, "That's not far enough."

He then proceeded to tell me that members of his current parish were taking a cruise to Alaska during the summer of 2009 to celebrate the parish's 150th anniversary. He asked me if I wanted to go to Alaska. At first, I thought he was joking. I'm extremely hydrophobic, and I thought he knew my fear of water was acutely worse than my fear of flying. I had never even let my sister convince me to ride in her boat in the Baltimore harbor. I couldn't imagine being on a ship in the middle of an ocean!

As the conversation at the dinner theater continued that evening, I realized Fr. Stefan was serious. He was very appreciative of the work I was doing for him and wanted a nice way to say thank you. I told him I'd think about it, although I really had no desire to go to Alaska, of all places. I love summer and hot weather. The thought of giving up ten days of warm Virginia weather to spend in chilly Alaska had no appeal for me.

My friends — who heard him make the offer — thought I was crazy to pass up such an opportunity. For the next two months, every time I saw Fr. Stefan, he would ask me again if I wanted to go to Alaska. I never gave him a definite answer.

Then, in February of 2009, I attended a healing Mass. Before Mass started, I was in the chapel praying when I heard someone enter the room and sit behind me. As I was kneeling there in the presence of Our Lord, I heard a voice behind me continually repeating, "Are you going to Alaska? Are you going to Alaska?" I felt like I couldn't say no. I turned around and told Fr. Stefan that I would go.

By the time I agreed to go, I had about five months of planning time before the actual trip, but I was nervous about the trip from the moment I told Fr. Stefan I would go. I love how Fr. Stefan is very nonchalant and "laid back" about all of his trips; I'm not like that. I'm a worrier. I need details, and I hate the unknown. I tend to play the "what-if?" game and get myself worked up over things that will most likely never happen:

What if I don't get my passport on time? (We had to fly into Vancouver.)

What if I get lost in the airport?

What if my luggage gets lost? Or even worse, what if the plane crashes?

What if the boat sinks? (Father actually suggested that I watch *Titanic* before the cruise!)

What if they don't have food I can eat to accommodate my restricted diet?

What will happen if the flight's delayed and we miss the boat?

And, of course, *Why did I let him talk me into this?!*

I put most of these thoughts out of my mind and worked on completing the manuscript. Our deadline for submission of the book was August 1, which was right in the middle of our scheduled trip. I knew the manuscript would need to be completed before flying to Alaska. Thankfully, as a teacher, I had off the month of July and was able to devote that time to completing the book. Being on the computer so much also permitted me to frequently check the weather in the different ports of Alaska we were scheduled to visit. I'm sure I probably told Fr. Stefan a dozen times how cold and rainy it was going to be in Alaska. He was convinced that I was wrong.

Just days after mailing the completed manuscript, our departure date had finally arrived. We were scheduled to leave Dulles International Airport at 6:45 on Sunday morning. I was traveling with Fr. Stefan, Colleen, and Dan, and began the morning with a 4:00 a.m. Mass and prayers for safe travel at their house prior to the drive to the airport. I was armed with my "stomach-friendly" comfort foods to help combat the anxiety and settle myself down.

Arriving at the airport, everything began smoothly until I tried to check in. My full name was too long to fit on the computer screen, and a warning came up that my ticket information did not match my passport. Luckily, the issue was quickly resolved, and we continued on through security.

Our next step was to get on the elevator to take a shuttle to our gate. As the four of us stepped into the elevator, a pilot joined us. As we talked with him, we discovered that he was flying to Dallas, Texas, at 6:45. He was our pilot!

We spent time chatting with him on the elevator and again in the shuttle. Father told him how this was my inaugural flight and how hesitant I was. He even tried to talk the pilot into moving our seats into first class — which, of course, he couldn't do. I'm glad we met the pilot, though, because I did feel a little less distraught after speaking with him and hearing his credentials. I'm sure our meeting was divine intervention!

Once on the plane and situated in our seats, I looked out the window. The sky looked dark with an approaching storm, and rain had already begun to hit the windows of our plane. The few days prior to our flight, the DC area had been hit with several electrical storms. I told Fr. Stefan that I hoped it wouldn't storm. With a smile he replied, "I hope it does storm. It will be more fun!" He also hoped we would hit a lot of turbulence. His comments weren't helping me to relax very much before the flight!

However, once the plane was finally in the air, I discovered it wasn't so bad. Overall, the flight was pretty smooth. The weather cleared up, and I didn't fret so much. The landing was a little unnerving, but I survived and was not afraid to get on our connecting flight to Vancouver a few hours later.

About an hour into our second flight of the day, Fr. Stefan made the observation that on both flights I had a seat directly next to the wing of the plane. He used an analogy of God protecting us under his wing. I thought of one of my favorite songs, "On Eagles' Wings," as he made the reference, and I was immediately comforted with the thought of God's promise for protection in Psalm 91. It was at that moment that I noticed the eagle logo on the wing of the American Airlines plane.

Upon arriving in Vancouver, we made our way to the hotel, and then went out to explore the city for the evening. One of the first attractions we noticed was a colorful statue of an eagle, which made us think of the reference made on the plane. As we continued to stroll through Vancouver, we saw many more of the splendidly painted eagle statues and knew they were a sign from God.

We began the next morning with Mass in the hotel room before leisurely making our way through town to catch a glimpse of our ship at the port. The thought of being on board and encompassed by water had my stomach once again tied in knots. Luckily, we still had a few hours before we would be permitted to board the ship. I was content keeping my feet on solid ground.

However, the time eventually came to board the ship. We were some of the earliest passengers to arrive, and I knew we still had several hours before the ship would set sail. Knowing that we were still docked kept my nerves somewhat under control. I had time to go to my stateroom and to explore the ship a bit before meeting others for lunch.

We were scheduled to sail at 5:00 p.m. Almost everyone was on the upper decks enjoying the sail-away party when the captain announced from the bridge that our sail-away time was being delayed until 8:00 that evening for some tests to be performed on the boat. He assured us that the tests had nothing to do with the safety of the ship. I wasn't convinced — but neither did I mind having a few more hours near land.

Since we were not sailing away at the sail-away party, several of us decided to go have dinner. After dining, we went to see one of the shows being performed at the ship's theater. The performance was scheduled to begin at 8:00, and since I had no view of the outside from the ship's theater, I forgot about the possibility of us setting sail. I enjoyed the show without a bit of worry.

At the end of the show, Fr. Stefan reported that he felt the ship moving. I was glad that I had not felt it. We eventually made our way to the outside area of the ship. We were no longer close to shore, but we had an amazing view of mountains on the horizon just as the sun was beginning to set. I walked right up to the edge of the ship and looked straight down. Bad idea! I backed up and tried not to think about what *could* go wrong. Instead, I chose to focus on the beautiful scenery surrounding us. I began snapping pictures and talking with some of the other passengers.

I met a lady named Maria, who was also part of the group from church. I learned that this was her first cruise as well; she, too, was afraid of the water. Now, I felt like I had something in common with someone. (I'm sure not many hydrophobic people go on cruises to have a good time!) I stuck with Maria, and we overcame our fear of being on the boat together.

We began each day that week with Mass. It seemed that the readings that week were perfectly chosen by God for people going on a cruise to Alaska. Most of the readings mentioned the sea or the mountains.

On our first full day at sea, the waters were rather rough. I could see the white peaks on the waves and feel the ship's rocking movement as I tried to walk about. As I nervously watched the waves, a Scripture passage came to my mind. I thought of the disciples in the boat during the storm while Jesus was asleep. They awakened Jesus, and he calmed the storm. I just kept envisioning Jesus lulling the waves and allaying my fears. The reading for that evening in the *Magnificat*, a monthly book of daily Scripture readings, was the story of Jesus walking on the water. One of the intercessions listed that evening said, "For those who *travel* and work upon the sea, protect them from harm."

After that evening, I was no longer afraid on the boat. I still got a bit "seasick" with the motion, but whenever the waves became choppy, I thought back to the passage in the Bible and felt much better.

I know that God answered a lot of prayers that week. Prior to leaving, I did a lot of research on the type of weather to expect at each port. According to weather.com, we should have had high temperatures in the 50s or lower 60s, with rain almost every day. When we arrived in Vancouver, however, the temperature was in the upper 80s. Our cab driver told us it was the warmest day Vancouver had seen since the early 1990s. Each port we stopped at had gorgeous weather in the 70s and low 80s all week. We didn't see a drop of rain while we were on the cruise. Visibility was perfect, and we were able to view glaciers from the ship that are not normally visible through the fog. All the local residents continually told us how unusual the weather had been for the week.

We disembarked for the final time at Whittier, where we took a tour bus to our final destination — Anchorage. As with each city we had visited earlier in the week, Anchorage was also experiencing a heat wave. Fr. Stefan wouldn't let me forget how worried I was that Alaska would be cold. He jokingly remarked to me that he wished he had packed warmer clothes. (I think he may have actually been the only one in our group who brought summer clothes.)

After locating our hotel in Anchorage, we met up with Megan, Fr. Stefan's "sister," who lives there. She took us out for lunch and then showed us around Anchorage. Father shared with Megan how part of her story was written in the book. As he was discussing the book with her, and how important her story was for the birth of the Paul Stefan Homes, he realized that yet another circle was complete. When I was first inspired by the idea that he should write a book and give the proceeds to the Paul Stefan Foundation, I didn't even know Megan's story. Through the process of writing this book, I learned how Megan's story was instrumental in the creation of these homes. And just a little over one week from mailing the completed manuscript to the publisher, I had the honor of meeting this wonderful young woman in person.

Megan took two days off from work to show us the beautiful sights around us. She drove us over four and a half hours to Denali National Park, where we saw beautiful Mt. McKinley, the tallest mountain in North America. Fr. Stefan celebrated Mass that afternoon on a picnic table in the shadow of Mt. McKinley. Nine hours in the car was worth this breathtaking sight. Thank you, Megan, for this wonderful experience.

After Mass in the park, we began our four-and-a-half-hour drive back to Anchorage to catch our flight home. With less than an hour left to drive, the skies opened up and it rained for the first time since we had been in Alaska. We couldn't have asked for a better trip.

Megan dropped us off at the airport two hours prior to our 9:00 p.m. flight. As we were waiting in line to check in, I told Fr. Stefan I wasn't nervous about flying anymore.

Upon boarding the plane, Fr. Stefan noticed right away that my seat was again directly by the wing. I knew that meant God was protecting me. We flew through the night on a crowded plane and landed in Dallas about 6:00 a.m. Our final flight home left Dallas at 8:00 that morning, and you guessed it — my seat was again by the wing of the plane, just *slightly* in front of the wing. It reminded me of learning how to ride a bike. When I first started learning to ride a bike, my dad held on to the bike to keep me from falling. Once I trusted, he let go, but he was always close enough behind to catch me if I got nervous again. God knew I trusted now, but I knew he was there if I ever doubted.

We experienced quite a bit of turbulence on the last leg of the trip, but after being awake for over thirty hours, maybe I was just too tired to let it bother me. I knew that his wing was there to protect me.

Fr. Stefan told me later that was about as bad as turbulence ever gets. If that's the case, I think I can handle it. I am grateful that Fr. Stefan convinced me to go on this trip to help me overcome my fears. Thank you, Father, for your kindness and generosity! When he asked me if I'd fly again, I told him I would. And even better than that — both Maria and I are excited about planning future cruises.

Bon Voyage!

Prayer for the Paul Stefan Home

I pledge to pray five Our Fathers, Hail Marys, and Glory Bes for the intentions of the Paul Stefan Home, especially for mothers and their babies.

Consecration to Our Lady of Guadalupe

I consecrate myself to Our Lady of Guadalupe, who is our mother. I am your child, and you are my mother. May you wrap us all in your mantle of love. I open my heart to you today, confident that you hear my prayers. I know that there is no reason to be afraid, anxious, or worried with our most precious mother holding me close to Her Heart. Mother Mary, thank you for bringing my prayers to Jesus and placing me in His arms close to His Sacred Heart.

Paul Stefan Home for Unwed Mothers
1-866-906-MOMS
www.paulstefanhome.org

BIBLIOGRAPHY

Cantalamessa, Raniero. *Life in the Lordship of Christ* (Kansas City, MO: Sheed and Ward, 1990).

Gesy, Lawrence J. *The Hem of His Garment: True Stories of Healing* (Huntington, IN: Our Sunday Visitor, 1996).

Gujski, Robert. *Diary of St. Maria Faustina Kowalska: Divine Mercy in My Soul* (http://www.faustina.ch/index_en.htm, accessed November 26, 2008).

Diary of St. Maria Faustina Kowalska: Divine Mercy in My Soul (Stockbridge, MA: Marians of the Immaculate Conception, 1987).

Martin, Ralph. *The Catholic Church at the End of an Age: What is the Spirit Saying?* (San Francisco: Ignatius Press, 1994).

Martin, Thérèse. *Story of a Soul: The Autobiography of St. Thérèse of Lisieux (Third Edition)*. Translated by John Clarke, O.C.D. (Washington, DC: ICS Publications, 1996).

Otto, Rudolf. *The Idea of the Holy*. Translated by John W. Harvey (New York: Oxford University Press, 1968).

Shaw, Steve. *Overview of Medjugorje* (http://www.medjugorje. org/overview.htm, accessed November 26, 2008).

The Our Lady of Victory Institutions (http://www.ourlady-ofvictory.org/FatherBaker/Welcome.html, accessed November 26, 2008).

For more information on Fr. Stefan or the Paul Stefan Foundation, please visit: www.paulstefanhome.org and www.fatherstefan.com.

For a copy of the novenas mentioned in this book, please visit:
http://www.divinemercysunday.com/novena.htm
http://www.ewtn.com/Thérèse/novena.htm
http://www.catholicdoors.com/prayers/novenas/p00098.htm

Notes